A Study Guide on the Best-Selling Book

YOUR WORK MATTERS TO GOD

DOUG SHERMAN AND WILLIAM HENDRICKS

NAVPRESS

A MINISTRY OF THE NAVIGATORS
P.O. BOX 6000, COLORADO SPRINGS, COLORADO 80934

© 1988 by Doug Sherman and William Hendricks
All rights reserved, including translation
ISBN 08910-92269

Printed in the United States of America

CONTENTS

Introduction

Perhaps you're familiar with cars that have what's called a turbo-charger on them. A standard car with a standard engine can do a pretty good job of moving you around town. But take almost any car and put a turbocharged engine on it, and watch out! Compared with the standard model, a turbocharged version will be an absolute screamer!

This discussion guide is meant to act like a turbocharger for our book, *Your Work Matters to God*. By itself, we think that book does an adequate job of explaining why God has given us work, and how we're to be distinctive in it. And if you're a fairly "high-octane" reader with a lot of initiative to apply biblical truth to your life, the book will probably get you a long way down the road toward Christlikeness in your work.

But we believe that most readers of our book would benefit enormously if, in addition to reading it, they had a way of applying its message to their unique situations. That's why we've "turbo-charged" our book by writing this discussion guide. Using it as a companion to what you read, you'll enjoy several high-performance benefits such as,

1. Seeing God's truth actually make a difference in your life. You don't need a lot of abstract theory. You want something that applies directly to your world. This guide can help to make biblical truth about work vital and real for *you*!
2. Finding fresh, practical ideas and strategies for how to live

out your faith on the job. The work world today is much different than it was just twenty years ago. And it continues to change daily. So you need creative, state-of-the-art approaches to living a Christlike lifestyle. This guide can help to stimulate your thinking in new and innovative ways.

3. Increased challenge and motivation for working with ethical integrity. The pressures toward compromise are enormous in today's marketplace. But using this guide regularly will inject a needed dosage of moral courage to help you stand strong. Furthermore, using it with a group of peers will enlist moral cheerleaders who will encourage you to maintain your ethical edge.

4. Insight into the issues you encounter each day. Faced with a deluge of tension, opportunities, problems, successes, dilemmas, breakthroughs, frustrations, and achievements, it's easy to feel swamped emotionally, intellectually, and spiritually. How can you sort it all out? This guide allows you to think through the complexities of your world and gain biblical perspective and direction.

5. Friends! Do you feel an "ethical loneliness" where you work? Do you feel like you're the only person who asks the questions you ask and values the things you value? If so, using this discussion guide with a group of your peers will open up a whole new level of relationships. In fact, many who have been this way before report that this process has introduced them to their first real friends.

These are ambitious claims! But we wouldn't make them if we hadn't seen many, many people benefit from the process we've designed in this guide.

SPECIAL FEATURES

This study guide is a bit different from others you've used before, for the following reasons:

Use of case histories.
One of the best ways to get at the heart of an issue is to discuss how it affects a real-life situation. Besides, it's always more interesting to talk about real people than dry theory. You will be

amazed at how much insight you gain into your own beliefs and values by looking at the lives of others, and by discussing their situations—and yours—with your group.

Open-ended questions.
We have tried to avoid asking questions that have obvious, simple answers. Instead, we want you to think about the issues raised in our book. Consequently, you'll have to talk a lot about yourself and your perspectives as you interact with this guide and with your group.

An emphasis on life-change.
The missing link in most Bible teaching today is the *application* of God's truth to our lives. The goal in this guide is not that you know our book thoroughly. Rather, our goal is that the simple truth that your work matters to God will make a real difference in how you live and work. That's why so many sessions ask you to *do* something in light of what's been discussed.

An applicational use of Scripture.
A useful and popular way to study the Bible is to begin with a scripture text, study it until you understand what it means, and then look for ways to apply that passage to life. In this guide you'll take the opposite approach: You will start with a major category of life—work—and the many issues raised by work. After examining those issues and how they affect you, you'll consider some biblical principles and apply those to the issues at hand. The Bible is definitely the backbone of our approach. But again, our emphasis in this guide is on life-change, not more Bible knowledge.

GET THE MOST FROM THIS GUIDE

To make full use of this resource, we have a number of suggestions.

Use it with a group.
We find that small discussion groups are an ideal way to apply biblical truth to life. That's why we've designed this as a *discussion* guide. We want you to interact over workplace issues with a group of your associates.

To have an effective group, you'll need to do several things:

1. Limit the group's size to six or eight people. If you have nine or more, we recommend splitting into two groups.
2. Make sure each participant has a copy of the book and a copy of this discussion guide.
3. Be clear as to the time and place for the discussion.
4. Clarify expectations up front. Everyone should agree on the purpose of the group and the level of commitment to it before you get started.
5. Set a termination date for the group, or a least for using this book; don't ask people for open-ended commitments. We've designed optional time frames for using this guide (see page 10).
6. Appoint a discussion leader. This person is not a teacher, but someone who can facilitate a healthy group interaction. (Suggestions for the leader are found on pages 9-10.)
7. Keep the discussion focused. The questions and material in this guide have been designed very carefully to help you think and talk about important issues. Avoid rabbit trails. And make sure *everyone* participates. This is a discussion, not a lecture or a platform for one person's point of view.
8. Come prepared to discuss. The preparation involved is minimal. Each session corresponds to a chapter in the book, so reading the chapter ahead of time will help. However, you can easily participate in the discussion even if you *haven't* read the chapter. Our concern is more about applying God's truth to your life and work than about getting you to read our book. It is a good idea, though, to read the material in the session before you meet. Group members will benefit from reading all the case studies in a session even if you discuss only one of them. Finally, you may find it helpful to mull over the questions before your meeting.
9. We haven't left much space in this guide to write many notes, so you may find it helpful to record answers to some questions in a separate notebook or journal. This will prove especially helpful for the exercises that require extended responses and reflection.
10. Some of the questions in this guide ask for painfully honest disclosure. For example, the workstyle inventory in session 2 asks you to tell the group about one area of your working life in which your attitudes fall short of God's standards. To make

this kind of vulnerability possible and healthy, you must agree to maintain strict confidences, to avoid judgment, and to strive for honesty even when it's uncomfortable.

SUGGESTIONS FOR GROUP LEADERS

You have an important role to play in making this experience helpful for everyone. In any group situation, someone's got to get things rolling and keep things moving. That's your job! If you do it well, the other natural dynamics of the group process will take care of everything else.

1. Come prepared. At a minimum, this involves reading the book and previewing the particular session that your group will cover. Doing so will give you confidence and a sense of where things are headed during the discussion. Moreover, your preparation sets a critical example for the other participants. It tells them how seriously you take the group, and therefore, how seriously they should take it.

2. In preparation for some of the sessions, you'll need to select from among several case studies and exercises the ones that are closest to your group's situation. For instance, in session 1, you probably won't have time to discuss Al's, Susan's, and Diane's situations in one meeting. Instead, choose the one case that seems most relevant to your group. On the other hand, be sure to allow enough time to discuss adequately the questions under "Ten Needs," because they bring the session to its resolution.

3. Your goal is to keep a lively discussion going. You can do that by probing people's responses, asking for clarification, and playing the devil's advocate. Of course, others in the group should be encouraged to do the same. Whatever you do, avoid "teaching" the content of the book.

4. Don't let someone dominate the group with his or her opinions or personality. You may have to referee at times. Also, try to get each participant—especially shy or quiet ones—to say at least one or two things at each session.

5. Keep track of the time. Before the group meets, think through how much time should be allotted to each section of the session. That way you can keep things moving. We've

designed each session to have resolution and completion, so if the last few questions or exercises are not covered, people may feel a bit frustrated. By the way, the ideal length of time for a discussion is about an hour.

6. End the discussion on time. People have other responsibilities and commitments. If the session lasts too long, they may develop a negative attitude toward the group. By contrast, cutting off a lively interaction will bring everyone back with enthusiasm. Our rule is, "Leave them longing, not loathing!"

POSSIBLE TIME PLANS

As we designed this discussion guide, we realized that not everyone can afford to go through all sixteen chapters. If the average group meets weekly to discuss one session, that would involve a sixteen-week commitment. That's ideal for some groups, but too long for others. Two shorter plans are listed below. Feel free to adapt the plans to the needs and interests of your group.

Six-session plan
1. Session 1
2. Session 5
3. Session 6
4. Session 9
5. Your choice of sessions 10-14
6. Sessions 15 and 16 combined

Twelve-session plan
1. Session 1
2. Session 2
3. Sessions 3 and 4 (your choice or combined)
4. Session 5
5. Session 6
6. Sessions 7 and 8 combined
7. Session 9
8. Your choice of sessions 10-14
9. Your choice of sessions 10-14
10. Your choice of sessions 10-14
11. Your choice of sessions 10-14
12. Sessions 15 and 16 combined

THIS GUIDE CAN BE USED FOR SELF-STUDY

Discussion groups won't work for everyone. That's okay. You can still enjoy valuable benefits from this guide even in self-study. Just make a couple of adjustments.

1. You'll have to be much more self-disciplined since you won't have the built-in accountability of a group. We recommend that you determine a specific time and place to study. Then put that in your appointment book so you won't crowd it out with other commitments.
2. Since you won't have a group to discuss the material with, you'll spend a great deal of effort in personal reflection and thought. Writing (or dictating) will replace discussing. However, you should seek opportunities to discuss your ideas with others—coworkers, your spouse, other Christians in your network. These people will be invaluable in helping you gain perspective and offering you objective feedback, even though they will participate on an informal basis.

BETWEEN TWO WORLDS

The gap that exists today between the world of religion and the world of work is growing rapidly. Like most Christians, your work and faith may rarely come together. You might feel like you live in two worlds: Your work seems generally antagonistic toward your Christianity, and your Christian faith seems irrelevant at work.

This is a tragedy. Like millions of Christians, perhaps you go to work each day unaided and unchallenged by the Word of God. As a consequence, you miss out on one of the greatest truths of Scripture—that *your* work matters to God!

In this session, we want you to consider some of the ways in which work and faith ignore each other, and the unfortunate results. We also want you to evaluate your own situation and the extent to which Christ accompanies you to your job each day.

CASE STUDY: AL

Until six months ago, Al managed a convenience store. The position offered him a steady income. It also provided good job security, since the store was part of a national chain.

However, the store sold soft-core pornographic magazines. As a Christian, Al felt deeply disturbed about this, and about his participation in it. He was especially disturbed by the older boys from a nearby high school who purchased the magazines to show their friends.

Day after day, Al's conscience bothered him. Finally, after

hearing a rousing message against pornography on a radio program, he turned in his resignation to the company, explaining his reasons for leaving.

Al thought that he would soon find a similar job with another chain. After all, he reasoned that God would reward his integrity by providing a new position—perhaps even a better position. Yet, six months later, Al was still out of work. He was also very frustrated.

He began contacting churches, Christian teachers, ministries, and even seminaries trying to find teaching on subjects like pornography, how to find God's will, and dealing with evil. Here and there, he found a few bits and pieces of insight. But for the most part, no one seemed to have answers that addressed his situation.

Now the company he worked for has offered his old job to him. He has explained to them that he doesn't want the position if he must sell the magazines. At the same time, he is out of money and feels he has a responsibility to provide for his family. With or without the magazines, Al is thinking about accepting the position again.

Discussion

1. Suppose Al came to you for help with this issue. What resources would you or could you offer him? Where would you send him for the insight and direction he needs?

2. Have you ever been in a situation similar to Al's? Where did you turn for answers?

3. Why do you think Christian teaching typically neglects to adequately address the issues of the workplace?

CASE STUDY: SUSAN

Susan is in management in a telemarketing firm. The company has been fairly successful marketing magazine subscriptions and the like. Susan's job entails hiring, training, and supervising the tele-marketing callers.

When she began the job, Susan's enthusiasm, drive, and personal skills on the phone immediately caught the eye of her supervisor. Consequently, she was given more and more responsibility over other employees. Her supervisor was especially interested in advancing her as a woman, since so many of the telemarketing callers were women.

But most of the other employees were not like Susan. Many came from lower-income backgrounds and had little education or experience in the sales environment. Others needed second jobs to supplement income. For the most part, these workers lacked enthusiasm and motivation. Consequently, there was a high turnover in the company, and supervision required high-pressure tactics.

Susan felt that as a Christian she had a responsibility to share the gospel with her coworkers. She began to build relationships with some of the employees.

One day she approached a woman named Cindy and initiated a conversation. "Cindy, your work is fine, but you don't seem to like your job very much. I'm wondering if there is anything I could do—any way I could help?"

Cindy eyed her with suspicion before faking a wry smile. "I got rent and three kids to pay for," she replied. "I work all day and then I come in here evenings. I do my quota. It's just a job, just a paycheck. Beyond that, I couldn't care less."

The conversation ended there. Susan went away feeling sad because Cindy's life seemed so empty, and frustrated because she had been unable to help.

Discussion

4. a. Do you know of many workers around you who feel the way Cindy feels? Describe their attitudes toward their jobs.

b. What are their attitudes toward religion?

5. Susan sincerely wants to help Cindy. But Cindy's perspective seems so dominated by her personal circumstances. What advice would you give Susan as she continues to work alongside Cindy?

6. Do you ever feel like your work is "just a job"? If so, why?

CASE STUDY: DIANE

"When I first met Diane she was a 34-year-old Mercedes-clad wife and careerist, juggling home and work, yet bored and dissatisfied with both. . . .

"She said she had been feeling troubled in recent months because she wasn't "holding it all together" the way she used to. I soon learned that she thought therapy would be a convenient way to rationalize her life and assuage her guilt. Though she wasn't fully aware of it at the time, she had been feeling guilty over having become a talented user of people, which helped in her profession, in the financial services area. Her husband was an ambitious lawyer who traveled a lot. She had begun filling the vacuum with new furniture, house renovations, clothes, and finally, affairs. Mostly short-lived, but longer than one-night stands; she felt she had her dignity to maintain.

"She was feeling anxious and depressed, which was often more acute in the evenings. What emerged was that she felt a sense of self-betrayal over the life she was leading and the values she had increasingly come to live by. . . .

"Problem was, she wasn't very happy. She gradually acknowledged that her work lacked meaning and challenge, and that she felt her life was basically empty. Nothing seemed to have much purpose or meaning beyond the immediate moment. She had no values that transcended the experience of daily life."[1]

Discussion

7. Diane appears to have it all—career prestige and success, financial success, a successful husband, freedom of time, and so on. Why do you think she is unhappy and feeling empty?

8. Do you know anyone like Diane? What values seem important to them?

9. If Diane were a coworker and she came to you for insight and direction, what would you tell her?

10. Do you think it's possible to be a committed Christian and also be successful in a career like Diane's? Why or why not?

WHY WORK?

"In nothing has the Church so lost her hold on reality as in her failure to understand and respect the secular vocation. She has allowed work and religion to become separate departments, and is astonished to find that, as a result, the secular work of the world is turned to purely selfish and destructive ends, and that the greater part of the world's intelligent workers have become irreligious, or at least, uninterested in religion. But is it astonishing? How can any one remain interested in a religion which seems to have no concern with nine-tenths of his life? The Church's approach to an intelligent carpenter is usually confined to exhorting him not to be drunk and disorderly in his leisure hours, and to come to church on Sundays. What the Church *should* be telling him is this: that the very first demand that his religion makes upon him is that he should make good tables."[2]

Discussion

11. Sayers says that the church has abandoned the arena of "secular vocation."

    a. Do you agree? If not, why not? If so, why has the church abandoned it?

    b. What is the result, in your opinion?

12. How might the church—including pastors, Christian leaders, and laypeople—begin to speak intelligently to the issues of the workplace? Or can it?

13. What one issue do you face on the job that you wish Christian teaching addressed more?

TEN NEEDS

The issue of faith and work is a raw, open nerve for many Christians. Perhaps it is for you. Perhaps one or more of the following expresses your situation:

1. You may go to work unaided and unchallenged by the Word of God.

2. You may be unclear as to how to take advantage of the resources of Christianity for day-to-day work problems and decisions.

3. You may be bored by your work and see no lasting value in it. Indeed, you may feel that only through your religious life do you find any purpose and meaning.

4. You may be skeptical as to the relevance of Christianity to the rigors of the secular work world.

5. You may struggle with the cost of integrity and need inspiration to keep your "ethical edge."

6. You may embarrass the cause of Christ by living an inconsistent lifestyle at work.

7. You may not be challenged to influence coworkers for Christ.

8. You may struggle with how to put work in its proper perspective and balance the many demands that compete for your time.

9. You may lack an integrated life purpose that spans the public and private arenas.

10. You may lack a sense of dignity in your day-to-day work, and thus your life.[3]

Discussion

14. Looking over the list of needs, which one most accurately expresses your situation?

15. Why is this area important to you?

16. In light of this what would you most like to gain as a result of going through this discussion guide? Explain your answer.

FOR FURTHER STUDY

Scripture

- Psalm 128—The psalmist describes the blessing that comes from honoring God in one's life and work.
- Colossians 3:17—This verse exhorts us to put Christ first in every aspect of our lives, including work. Also see 1 Peter 1:14-16.
- Hebrews 4:12-13—This passage describes the relevance of Scripture to the entirety of our lives. Also see Psalm 19:7-11.

Reading

Sayers, Dorothy. *Creed or Chaos?* London: Harcourt and Brace, 1949.
Terkel, Studs. *Working.* New York: Pantheon Books, 1974.
Yankelovich, Daniel. *New Rules.* Toronto: Bantam Books, 1982.

Projects

1. Poll some of your coworkers and associates, asking one or more of the following questions:

   - Do you think religion makes any difference in your work?
   - Where would you go to find biblical direction for workplace issues like stress, integrity, ambition, and relationships on the job?

• Have you ever heard a sermon, read a book, listened to a tape, or been to a seminar that related practical biblical principles to everyday work issues?

2. Ask your pastor or Sunday school teacher to briefly explain your church's view toward everyday work.
3. Show the list of ten needs on page 18 to other Christian laypeople you know. Which of these are needs for them?

4. Answer the following question (and submit your response to your pastor or Sunday school teacher if you'd like, or send it to us!): What one issue do you face all the time at work that you wish Christian teaching would address more?

NOTES: 1. Douglas LaBier, *Modern Madness: The Emotional Fallout of Success* (Reading, Mass.: Addison-Wesley Publishing Company, Inc., 1986), pages 25-36.
2. Dorothy Sayers, *Creed or Chaos?* (London: Harcourt and Brace, 1949), pages 56-57.
3. Doug Sherman and William Hendricks, *Your Work Matters to God* (Colorado Springs, Colo.: NavPress, 1987), pages 13-14.

GOING FOR IT!

In chapter 2 of *Your Work Matters to God* we describe a "secular" view of work. But there is no one secular view of work. Rather, a number of ideas and attitudes exist in today's workplace that are "secular" because they have one thing in common: *they all leave God out.*

If you leave out God and His Word and His will when you think about your work—about why you go to work, about your plans for your career, about how you deal with coworkers, about your ethics and integrity on the job, about the money you make, and so forth—you're looking at work from a *secular* point of view.

In the discussion that follows, we want you to evaluate your own attitudes toward work. Believe it or not, most Christians—even most committed Christians—base their attitudes and actions on some very secular ideas! Your goal should not be to discuss what a secular view of work is. Instead, we want you to talk about the ways it shows up in your own life.

CASE STUDY: TIM

Tim had been a hotshot at a prestigious East Coast business school. Prior to attending that school, he had worked for several years in junior management at a manufacturing plant near his hometown. Thanks to his experience plus his enviable degree and impressive recommendations, he had been selected by a Fortune 500 company for an excellent management position with an inflated salary and high expectations for a quick rise to upper-level leadership.

Several months into the new job, Tim got a call from a close friend from graduate school. "The gang's getting together up at Marcy's father's place in New Hampshire," he explained. "Sort of a reunion. Be there! We'll all compare notes!"

Tim enthusiastically accepted. On the appointed weekend, he drove up to New Hampshire, where his friends were waiting. After everyone had stuffed themselves on steamers and lobsters, they sat talking late into the night about their experiences since graduation.

Everyone agreed that Tim had gotten the best job.

"I can't believe they pay you what they do," remarked one person.

"Well they have to," replied Tim. "You know what it costs to live in Manhattan. Besides," he added sarcastically, "I'm worth it!"

His boast was met by a howl of derisive laughter and expletives.

"Yeah, well I thought you almost didn't take that job," said someone else after a moment.

"That's right," explained Tim. "It came down to this one or 3M. I had the two recruiters practically in a fist fight trying to lure me in. Frankly, the guy from 3M made a better case."

"So what made you pick this one?" he was asked.

"Greed!" blurted out someone else.

Again everyone laughed and nodded. Tim just smiled.

"It's like Michael Douglas said in *Wall Street*. Greed runs America. Greed is good!"

"It's true!" laughed Tim. "Corporate recruiting is just like an auction. You sell yourself to the highest bidder!"

Discussion

1. What is the obvious motivation for Tim as he thinks about his career?

2. Suppose Tim is a Christian. As long as he donates generously to his church and Christian organizations and charities, should anyone really care how much he makes and what he does with the money he keeps? Why or why not?

3. Suppose you and Tim get into a conversation about these issues and he challenges you by saying, "Okay, so you think my attitude is all wrong. Then tell me what sort of attitude I *should* have in my position." How would you respond?

4. Think about your own career and your motivations for work.

    a. To what degree are they similar to Tim's?

    b. To what extent is your response to question 3 influenced by your own situation?

CASE STUDY: ELIZABETH

Elizabeth looked tired. Even worse, she felt tired. Not just tired. Bone-tired. Exhausted. Burned out. Yet every morning, after dropping off her seven-year-old daughter at school and her three-year-old son at the daycare center, she managed to be at her desk in time to smile and offer a hearty "Good morning!" to her boss, a senior executive in a major tire company.

One morning her greeting was met with a request: "Elizabeth, can I see you in my office?" Her boss's tone seemed just a little too somber, she thought, and suddenly she felt a wave of anxiety.

After she closed the door and sat down, he began. "Elizabeth, I'm recommending that you set up an appointment with Dr. Zachary—you know—the, uh, psychologist for our company."

Elizabeth had always known that her boss wasn't one to beat around the bush. But this was an absolute bombshell!

"Dr. Zachary! What do I need to see him for? Is there something wrong with my work? I don't understand!"

"There's nothing wrong with your work. It's just—you seem like you're under a lot of stress these days, and . . . ."

"Well, yeah, I guess I am. But I'm handling it. And I think my work's been okay. Don't you? I mean, I've even been skipping lunch to keep up with the typing, and I stayed late again just last week!"

"I know, I know. But you also forgot my appointment with

the vice president. And you booked me through the Denver airport in February! Now those aren't major problems, I guess, but it just seems to me you're not always on top of things these days. I'm not asking you to see Dr. Zachary. I'm telling you."

So Elizabeth went. Dr. Zachary was an extremely polite man with a calming manner. Though she felt extreme apprehension when she walked in, she soon found herself chatting quite openly about herself in response to his gentle questioning.

She explained that her husband had left her a year earlier for a trial separation. He continued to send support for her and the children. But only a month ago he had told her he was planning to file for divorce. She could keep the house and one of the cars. He'd pay alimony, but he wanted out of the marriage.

She said that a number of her friends had had their husbands leave, too. She described the loneliness they all felt, and the guilt and the anger. She then talked about the affection she felt for her children, and how she intended to work hard to provide for them.

But she also admitted that she felt terribly weary, and sometimes wished she could run away from it all. "Not that I ever would, you understand," she said. "But sometimes I just want to do something for myself for a change."

"I can imagine you would, Elizabeth," Dr. Zachary replied. "From what you've told me, it sounds like you've lived most of your life for other people. Maybe you need to start living for yourself. In the end, the person you've got to please is not your husband, not your children, not even your boss, or this company, or your friends, or your parents—but you!

"If your work and your life aren't fulfilling to you, then you not only have a right to make some changes, but you have a responsibility to make them. You have to determine what works best for you. Are you willing to do that?"

Discussion
5. a. Dr. Zachary's advice is extremely common in the work world today. What truths do you see in his words?

    b. What dangers do you see in his counsel?

6. Elizabeth's back is against the wall in many ways. Facing the pressures she does, it's quite likely she will adopt much of Dr. Zachary's perspective. Where might this lead in the long run?

7. Suppose Elizabeth is a Christian. What perspective from her faith should she factor into the way she responds to her circumstances?

8. a. How about you? In what ways do you agree that when it comes to your job, "You have to determine what works best for you"?

   b. What value do you place on self-determination and self-fulfillment in your career?

CASE STUDY: FRED

Sitting in his well-worn, green plaid, wing chair, his feet stretched toward a crackling fire like a pair of cats, Fred sipped his third Scotch—or was it his fourth? Anyway, he kept bringing to mind the sights and sounds of the evening's banquet.

He'd sat at the head table for what seemed forever while they listed his accomplishments: his military background, his education, his early career in law, the big cases he'd won, his honors, the organizations he belonged to (and generously supported), his civic responsibilities, the articles and books he'd written, the boards on which he served.

On and on and on it went. With each one, he could almost hear the audience murmur in amazement. Yes, an impressive set of accomplishments.

He poured himself another Scotch and sat down.

The master of ceremonies introduced Fred's children. Except Marilee. Fortunately, they did not mention Marilee's name. It seemed appropriate. She was a no-account, the product of his second marriage—to that crazy woman who'd just been after his money. Thank God she'd died in a car accident after the divorce.

But Frederick, Jr., was there. Just out of law school. He was a good kid—a few strange ideas, but he'd soon learn how the world works. Give him some time on the street. Let him get kicked around. Maybe he'd even come back to his old man someday.

And Jeffrey, who had inherited his father's build, his instincts. The boy was destined for the pros, the way he was running the ball at USC. If he could just stay off the dope—and keep from getting into some stupid paternity suit! No common sense, that one.

And Elisa. The applause for her had seemed especially thunderous. Such a beautiful girl. So beautiful, but so mixed up. Seemed like he'd paid a fortune to that shrink, and still the girl wasn't right. Always depressed and withdrawn.

Fred shook his head as he thought about his kids, and swore as he dropped the cap to the second bottle. It rolled under the icebox. He let it go.

Then they introduced his wife. He'd smiled his way through, but snickered inside as they talked about her "faithful, loyal companionship" as a wife and mother. He couldn't stand the woman. Couldn't stand the way she looked, the way she talked, the way she acted. The one thing he had to hand to her, though, was that she'd done her best with those kids.

So he'd sat through all the introductions, and all the accolades from people like the mayor (who probably hated his guts) and the athletes (whose legal problems he'd taken care of, so they owed him lots of favors) and his minister (who was always asking for a donation it seemed) and his partners (who were about ready to sue him).

He'd sat there and sat there and listened to it all until he thought he'd die if he didn't get a drink. And finally—finally they got around to the presentation:

> "In recognition of his outstanding leadership as a devoted husband and father, in honor of his unswerving commitment to the high ideals that our society places on the family unit, and in appreciation of his exemplary contribution to the life and vitality of this community, the Family Council hereby proclaims Frederick H. Buchanan, Sr., as Father of the Year."

His head roared with the applause, roared like a thousand waterfalls, filling him with pride, with self-approval, and with tears. He raised his glass in a self-congratulatory toast, drained it out, and dozed off in the glow of the fire.

Discussion

9. Is Frederick H. Buchanan, Sr., a success? Why or why not?

10. How do we measure success in our culture?

11. What does success look like in your career or occupation?

12. a. To what extent are you pursuing the picture of success you described above?

    b. Why are you doing so?

YOUR WORKSTYLE: AN INVENTORY

Christians who take their faith seriously generally assume that *secular* is a word that describes someone else. Perhaps you feel that way. Perhaps you feel that because you attend church regularly, pray frequently, and live a basically good, moral life, you would be described more often as "religious" rather than "secular."

We would probably agree that you are religious. But some of the most religious people we know have some very secular ideas and attitudes governing their lives, especially about work. In fact, we find that *we also* have been strongly influenced by the secular culture around us, and are in a process of changing our minds to a more godly perspective!

The following inventory is a simple way to evaluate your attitudes and actions on the job—what we call your "workstyle." If your workstyle is less than godly, it's probably because your underlying beliefs and values are fairly secular—that is, they leave God out.

13. Evaluate your workstyle by quickly responding to each state-
ment and question. Don't picture yourself the way you think
you *ought* to be or would *like* to be, but rather the way you
actually *are*.

   a. I begin each work day with a prayer that God will help me
do my work in a Christlike way.
Never 1 2 3 4 5 6 7 8 9 10 Frequently

   b. If I saw that people in my company were going to do something in an unethical or illegal manner, I would stand up
and voice objections.
No way 1 2 3 4 5 6 7 8 9 10 Definitely

   c. I set limits to the amount of time and energy I put into my
job, and my schedule reflects those limits.
Never 1 2 3 4 5 6 7 8 9 10 Always

   d. I present the gospel message clearly to my coworkers.
Never 1 2 3 4 5 6 7 8 9 10 Frequently

   e. I would accept a job that paid extremely well, even if it
didn't fully utilize my abilities, over a job that might
thoroughly satisfy but didn't pay as well.
No way 1 2 3 4 5 6 7 8 9 10 Definitely

   f. I discuss how the Bible relates to workplace issues with
other Christians in my profession.
Never 1 2 3 4 5 6 7 8 9 10 Frequently

   g. I pray for my supervisor, my employer, my employees, my
customers, and others in my work world.
Never 1 2 3 4 5 6 7 8 9 10 Frequently

   h. I talk about the nature of my work and the issues I face on
the job to my spouse and my children.
Never 1 2 3 4 5 6 7 8 9 10 Frequently

   i. Have I ever . . .
      • pilfered supplies? Yes   No

- used the company phone to make personal long-distance phone calls? Yes No
- taken too much time for lunch? Yes No
- falsified or exaggerated information on a resumé? Yes No
- participated in a bribe or kickback? Yes No
- charged personal expenses on the company expense account? Yes No
- used marijuana, cocaine, speed, or other drugs on the job? Yes No
- cheated on my income tax? Yes No
- lied to a customer? Yes No
- called in sick when not sick? Yes No

Discussion

Chances are, you probably can identify at least two or three areas where your workstyle is far less than Christlike. Don't be discouraged! The point of this exercise is not to embarrass you or make you feel bad. Instead, we want to help you think about how God affects—or should affect—your work.

14. a. Select one item in which you feel you are not doing as well as you should. Explain why you think your attitude or behavior is not acceptable to God.

    b. What do you think would be a more Christlike workstyle?

15. Assuming that you can detect ways in which your view of work is fairly secular, why have you adopted this secular perspective? Some possible reasons follow; you can no doubt add some others.

    - "I guess my education presented life this way. I never questioned it."
    - "I've always assumed that religion is religion and business is business and shouldn't interfere with each other."
    - "I have no idea how my faith applies to day-to-day work situations."

16. What practical steps could you take to change your perspectives on work to a more godly point of view?

FOR FURTHER STUDY

Scripture
- Psalm 1—Pictures life with God and without God.
- Psalm 15—We call this "the business person's psalm." It describes what a godly character looks like in the arena where it's most needed—at work!
- Luke 12:15-21—The parable of the rich fool, a person whose life consisted only of his possessions.

Reading
LaBier, Douglas. *Modern Madness: The Emotional Fallout of Success.* Reading, Mass.: Addison-Wesley Publishing Company, Inc., 1986.

Projects
1. Read articles in *The Wall Street Journal* or other sources on the following individuals: Andrew Krieger, Ivan Boskey, Paul Tudar Jones II, and Donald Trump. Evaluate statements they have made and statements that have been made about them to determine their views on work. To what extent do you share their views? To what extent do you envy them?

2. Review the inventory on pages 28-29 with a Christian coworker. Then discuss ways in which you could help each other develop godly workstyles on the job.

YE CANNOT SERVE GOD AND MAMMON

The Two-Story view of work divides life into "sacred" and "secular" areas. It assumes that God is interested only in "sacred" things, religious things. Therefore, everyday work, which is "secular," doesn't really matter to Him.

This type of thinking is very common among Christians today. It even gets promoted by Christian teaching, not only by what is explicitly said, but also by what is left unsaid. Yet, despite its popularity and appealing logic, this view of work is sub-biblical.

In this session, we want to examine this Two-Story view of work and consider why it is unacceptable.

THE MISSIONARY'S TESTIMONY

Maybe you've heard testimonials similar to the one that follows:

> Thank you for the opportunity to speak on the issue of missions, and why I think every committed Christian should be involved in full-time service to God.
>
> Let me share with you a little bit of my background. Prior to attending seminary, I was a businessman involved in the sale of drill presses. These drill presses were used in some of the more sophisticated machine shops.
>
> During the early years of business, I realized it took a lot of time to get the business going, and that limited my involvement in church. But as time went on, I found more and more

of an interest in serving God. As I became more heavily
involved, I began to reflect on my life and what I was doing in
my day-to-day work. I became gripped by the fact that my
whole life was given to a business that puts holes in metal—
holes that are later filled up with screws!

The Things That Last

While I was thinking about this, I began to think of the
things that last for eternity. This was prompted by a sermon
my pastor gave one day on the two things that last for
eternity—the Word of God and the souls of men.

As I pondered the significance of these things, I began to
think about how meaningless my life was, given to making
holes in metal which will someday be filled up with screws.
Not only did this occupation seem meaningless, but the
thought dawned on me that someday the whole earth will be
destroyed, as it says in 2 Peter, and all the elements of the
earth will melt—if it doesn't rust before then! The utter futil-
ity of my life as a businessman led me to start considering the
ministry. I wanted to invest my life in things that will really
last.

As I thought of this, I began to think about some of the
frustrations I felt as a "part-time" servant of God. I was only
able to attend church and be involved in the program on
Wednesday nights, Sunday mornings, and Sunday nights. I
realized that I was not only part-time, but I was also serving
God only in my tired hours. And I felt He was worthy of something much more.

A Career Change

This led me to a very important decision concerning my
career. Was I going to have a life given principally to something as futile as putting holes in metal, or to something that
would really count? I began to consider what business is all
about, and I realized that my whole motive for being in business was self-centered. I was principally in it to provide an
income for myself and all the comforts I and my family
wanted. Ultimately, I realized that my orientation was one of
greed. I was just in it for myself.

Furthermore, I saw that I lived in a business culture

dominated by self-centered and greedy thinking. And I knew that I could not continue to be around it without picking up the same values that that culture had. Self-centered values oppose every line of the Bible. I knew I wanted to be different and to live a different lifestyle.

Well, as if these things had not been enough to convince me, the final thing that struck me was a challenge I heard from a prominent Christian leader. He told me that as a minister of the gospel, I had the highest calling on the face of the earth!

As I thought about this, I could see why he would say that. Without question, the program of God in the world today is to save sinners and to sanctify saints. Drilling holes in metal is far removed from that work. In fact, if I wanted to be on the front line as a participant in God's work, and not just a spectator, I needed to give my life work to the things that really count.

Because of these reasons, I chose to go into full-time work for God.

A Challenge
Today I would challenge you to do the same. Sometimes I think that the ministry is one of the ways God has of filtering out uncommitted people. It's like Jesus told the rich, young ruler: "Sell all and follow Me." I realize that some must stay behind and make enough money to support the full-time people. And I'm grateful for them. But the fact remains, full-time servants are on the cutting edge of God's work!

Well, what about you? *You* don't have to be addicted to mediocrity! *You* don't have to live a half-hearted commitment to Christ! Jesus said in John 6:27, "Do not work for the food which perishes, but for the food which endures to eternal life." This is our Savior's exhortation to make our lives count! In light of this admonition, I challenge you to surrender yourself to a full-time life of service and ministry.[1]

Discussion
1. How does listening to this missionary's challenge make you feel?

2. Have you ever heard similar remarks made by someone in
   "full-time" Christian ministry? How did that experience make
   you feel about your "secular" job?

3. What aspects of the missionary's thinking, if any, do you find
   biblical, healthy, and valuable?

4. What aspects of his outlook, if any, do you think are unbiblical, unrealistic, or unhealthy?

BIBLE STUDY

There are many, many scripture passages we could use to refute
the Two-Story view of work. One excellent passage to consider is
Ephesians 6:5-9:

> Slaves, be obedient to those who are your masters according
> to the flesh, with fear and trembling, in the sincerity of your
> heart, as to Christ; not by way of eyeservice, as men-pleasers,
> but as slaves of Christ, doing the will of God from the heart.
> With good will render service, as to the Lord, and not to men,
> knowing that whatever good thing each one does, this he will
> receive back from the Lord, whether slave or free. And, mas-
> ters, do the same things to them, and give up threatening,
> knowing that both their Master and yours is in heaven, and
> there is no partiality with Him.

5. In the passage from Ephesians, the Apostle Paul urges
   employees to obey their employers just as they would obey
   Christ. If Jesus Christ were your Boss, how would that affect
   the way you do your job?

6. a. According to the passage, how should you serve your employer?

   b. Explain how this would affect the way you do your job.

7. You spend most of your time, use much, if not most, of your emotional energy, and probably apply most of your skills and abilities at work. Therefore, it seems reasonable to conclude that in handing out rewards, the Lord will look carefully at your work. What will He reward in *your* work life? (If you doubt that God will reward everyday work, see Colossians 3:23-25.)

8. Ephesians 6:5-9 suggests that if you supervise someone, you will be evaluated and rewarded in light of that responsibility. (That's what the phrase "no partiality" implies.) What standards would you expect God to have for your job?

9. This passage says that as you work you should do the will of God from your heart. In your opinion, how does your work fulfill God's will?

FOR FURTHER STUDY

Scripture
- 1 Corinthians 15:35-53—Paul discusses the nature of the body as it exists now and as it will exist in eternity. Also see 2 Corinthians 5:1-10.
- Colossians 3:17—The verse implies that there is no distinction to be made between the "secular" and the "sacred."

- 2 Peter 3:8-18—Peter explains what sort of people Christians ought to be in the present, in light of our future in eternity.
- Revelation 1:6—This verse affirms that we are all priests before God.

Reading
Peabody, Larry. *Secular Work Is Full-Time Service.* Fort Washington, Pa.: Christian Literature Crusade, 1974.

Projects
1. Read a missionary biography and evaluate the extent to which the subject of the book held a Two-Story view of work and life.
2. Ask three Christian laypeople why they are in "secular" work as opposed to going into the ministry "full-time."
3. Ask a seminary student why he is training for the ministry as opposed to going into a "secular" career.

NOTE: 1. Doug Sherman and William Hendricks, *Your Work Matters to God* (Colorado Springs, Colo.: NavPress, 1987), pages 43-45.

THE STRATEGIC SOAPBOX

In session 3 we read the testimony of a missionary who articulated a Two-Story view of life and work. Another attitude toward work that is popular among Christians today is the Mainstream Model, which says that work is primarily a platform for believers to use in presenting the gospel. Christians need to participate in the "mainstream" of the culture—especially work—in order to rub shoulders with nonChristians. However, the work itself is of little importance; it is simply a platform, and it helps to pay the bills.

Unfortunately, this view, like the Two-Story view, is also sub-biblical. Certainly Christians need to use work as a platform for evangelism. But God intends for your job to be *much* more than that.

In this session, we want you to evaluate the Mainstream view of work and think about some purposes for work in addition to evangelism. Let's begin by hearing from Larry, an enlisted man in the military.

THE SOUL-WINNER

Let me begin by saying I'm not a speaker or a preacher or anything. So you'll understand if I'm a bit nervous.

But since this is missions Sunday, the pastor asked me to talk about how each of us as a Christian is really a missionary, right where we are. As we've heard from a number of speakers, Jesus said, "Go and make disciples." That means we need to share the gospel, whether it's with the guy who lives next door or someone who lives on the other side of the world.

So that's our job as Christians—to be soul winners. It's like I heard someone say once: "Jesus' last command must be our first concern."

So really, even though I'm up here in a uniform and I'm paid by Uncle Sam, my real Boss is Jesus Christ. My real job is sharing the gospel with other guys. Being in the service gives me a great way to do that.

You might feel like saying, "Well Larry, if you feel that way, why don't you get out of the service and go into the ministry?" But you see, this job *is* my ministry! It gives me a super platform for sharing my faith, and that's what it's all about.

Let me explain. Being out there with lots of nonChristians, on their turf, I find tons of ways to talk about the Lord. Just the other day, me and this other guy had to go pick up an officer at the federal building downtown. So on our way, we passed this church that had a sign for a motto or a verse or something.

Well, this sign read, "Seven days without prayer makes one weak!" Y'know, weak—w-e-a-k—instead of w-e-e-k! So I read that out loud to this guy. Then I said, "Boy, that's for sure!" I was trying to get a response out of him, you see.

And he says, "Whaddya mean?"

So I explained to him about prayer, and how Christians can talk with God any time. It was a great chance to be a witness.

Of course, I think it's not just what you say that counts, but how you live. As you know, there're lots of rules and regulations in the service. And the officers are constantly watching to see whether you're doing things right. So I try to be real careful how I perform. I mean, if I mess up in my assignments, then it just reflects badly on my testimony.

And y'know, I may be the only Christian some of these guys ever meet. Imagine if I didn't tell them about Christ. Or imagine if, because of me, somebody didn't trust Christ. If he died and went to hell, man, I think God would hold me responsible! So I try to use every chance I have to witness.

Now maybe you're sitting out there saying, "Well, Larry, that's great for you. But what about me?" Well, Jesus is calling you to be a soul-winner, too. Like I said before, every Christian is really a missionary

And we all gotta do it right where we are. Maybe you work in a bank or an office. I know a lot of people in this church work over at the factory. Well, you may think you're there just to earn a living for your family or something. But the way I see it, God's really paying you to talk to other people who need to hear the gospel. That's not a bad deal, huh—getting paid to do God's work!

Now you may be thinking, *I'm scared to talk about the Lord! People will think I'm weird, or they'll tell me to get lost.*

Well, maybe. But that's never happened to me. The guys in my unit know I'm a Christian. I talk a lot about the Lord. I talked with my commanding officer about it one day, and he basically said that as long as it doesn't interfere with my work or cause problems with the other guys, he doesn't care. "It's a free country," he said.

And besides, even if somebody does think you're weird or something, that's okay. A lot of people thought Jesus was weird, too, y'know! You gotta take a stand for the Lord sometime. After all, He said, "If you deny Me on earth, I'll deny you in Heaven."

Well, I just want to close with this one thought. A guy told me once, "Larry, you don't really have anything to live for until you've got something to die for." Well, Jesus is worth dying for. And so my reason for living is to tell people about Him. I don't know what you're living for, but if you're not living to be a soul-winner, then you're not really living. Jesus was willing to die for you. I hope you're ready to die for Him.

Discussion

1. How does listening to Larry's challenge make you feel? Motivated? Guilty? Angry?

2. Have you ever heard someone make similar remarks? How did that make you feel . . .

   about your job?

   about evangelism?

3. What aspects of Larry's thinking do you agree with, if any?

4. Are there aspects of Larry's view that you think are unbiblical, unrealistic, or unhealthy? If so, what are they?

FOR FURTHER STUDY

Scripture

- Compare the five versions of the Great Commission recorded in Scripture (Matthew 28:18-20, Mark 16:15-18, Luke 24:44-49, John 20:19-23, Acts 1:4-8). Considered together, what does Jesus want His followers to do with their lives?

- 1 Peter 1:18-25, 2:13-17, 4:12-19—Peter's exhortations regarding the link between our lifestyle and our testimony.

Reading

DeMoss, Ted and Robert Tamasy. *The Gospel and the Briefcase.* Wheaton, Ill.: Tyndale House Publishers, 1984.

Packer, J.I. *Evangelism and the Sovereignty of God.* Downers Grove, Ill.: InterVarsity Press, 1979.

Petersen, Jim. *Living Proof.* Colorado Springs, Colo.: NavPress, 1989.

Projects

1. Find a Christian who you think has done a good job of integrating his faith with his work. Ask how he presents the gospel on the job.
2. Ask a nonChristian coworker how he has felt when Christians have presented the gospel to him or to others.

YOUR WORK MATTERS TO GOD

In chapter 5 of *Your Work Matters to God,* we argue that work has inherent dignity and value, based on three important biblical principles:

1. God is a Worker.
2. God created people as workers.
3. God created people to be His coworkers.

In this session we want to accomplish two things. First, we want you to understand that the Bible clearly teaches these three principles, and thus establishes that everyday work is significant. Second, we want you to start applying these truths to *your* work, so that you will see that your work matters deeply to God.

GOD IS A WORKER

Many, many passages describe the work that God does. We'll consider only one, Psalm 104 (TLB). In this psalm, we find a "travelogue" of the Creation, which shows the incredible work of God. Read the psalm out loud.

> I bless the Lord: O Lord my God, how great you are! You are robed with honor and with majesty and light! You stretched out the starry curtain of the heavens, and hollowed out the surface of the earth to form the seas. The clouds are his char-

iots. He rides upon the wings of the wind. The angels are his messengers—his servants of fire!

You bound the world together so that it would never fall apart. You clothed the earth with floods of waters covering up the mountains. You spoke, and at the sound of your shout the water collected into its vast ocean beds, and mountains rose and valleys sank to the levels you decreed. And then you set a boundary for the seas, so that they would never again cover the earth.

He placed springs in the valleys, and streams that gush from the mountains. They give water for all the animals to drink. There the wild donkeys quench their thirst, and the birds nest beside the streams and sing among the branches of the trees. He sends rain upon the mountains and fills the earth with fruit. The tender grass grows up at his command to feed the cattle, and there are fruit trees, vegetables and grain for man to cultivate, and wine to make him glad, and olive oil as lotion for his skin, and bread to give him strength. The Lord planted the cedars of Lebanon. They are tall and flourishing. There the birds make their nests, the storks in the firs. High in the mountains are pastures for the wild goats, and rock-badgers burrow in among the rocks and find protection there.

He assigned the moon to mark the months, and the sun to mark the days. He sends the night and darkness, when all the forest folk come out. Then the young lions roar for their food, but they are dependent on the Lord. At dawn they slink back into their dens to rest, and men go off to work until the evening shadows fall again. O Lord, what a variety you have made! And in wisdom you have made them all! The earth is full of your riches.

There before me lies the mighty ocean, teeming with life of every kind, both great and small. And look! See the ships! And over there, the whale you made to play in the sea. Every one of these depends on you to give them daily food. You supply it, and they gather it. You open wide your hand to feed them and they are satisfied with all your bountiful provision.

But if you turn away from them, then all is lost. And when you gather up their breath, they die and turn again to dust.

Then you send your Spirit, and new life is born to replenish all the living of the earth. Praise God forever! How he must rejoice in all his work! The earth trembles at his glance; the mountains burst into flame at his touch.

I will sing to the Lord as long as I live. I will praise God to my last breath! May he be pleased by all these thoughts about him, for he is the source of all my joy. Let all sinners perish—all who refuse to praise him. But I will praise him. Hallelujah!

Discussion

1. List as many "occupations" of God as you can find represented in this psalm (for example, farmer).

2. Describe some additional work that God does that the psalmist did not mention.

3. How does thinking about the specific ways in which God works affect the way you regard the world of everyday work, where you spend your time?

GOD CREATED PEOPLE AS WORKERS

Read Genesis 1:26-27 aloud:

Then God said, "Let Us make man in Our image, according to Our likeness; and let them rule over the fish of the sea and over the birds of the sky and over the cattle and over all the earth, and over every creeping thing that creeps on the earth."

And God created man in His own image, in the image of God He created him; male and female He created them.

Discussion

4. In what ways do people "rule over" the creation?

5. As you think about your own job and industry, what aspect of
the world do you "rule over"?

GOD CREATED PEOPLE TO BE HIS COWORKERS

Read Psalm 8 aloud:

O LORD, our Lord,
How majestic is Thy name in all the earth,
Who hast displayed Thy splendor above the heavens!
From the mouth of infants and nursing babes Thou hast
established strength,
Because of Thine adversaries,
To make the enemy and the revengeful cease.

When I consider Thy heavens, the work of Thy fingers,
The moon and the stars, which Thou hast ordained;
What is man, that Thou dost take thought of him?
And the son of man, that Thou dost care for him?
Yet Thou hast made him a little lower than God,
And dost crown him with glory and majesty!
Thou dost make him to rule over the works of Thy hands;
Thou hast put all things under his feet,
All sheep and oxen,
And also the beasts of the field,
The birds of the heavens, and the fish of the sea,
Whatever passes through the paths of the seas.

O LORD, our Lord,
How majestic is Thy name in all the earth!

Discussion

6. Psalm 8 speaks of the *work* of God. Who oversees the work of
God on earth?

7. Describe the nature of your job responsibilities. In what ways does your work match work that God Himself does? In other words, what does God do that you also do in your job? Some examples follow:

   - "God stands for justice and contends with evil. I do the same in my job as a policeman."
   - "God creates and designs. I do the same in my job as a graphic designer."
   - "God nurtures the growth of His creatures. I do the same in my work as a mother."

8. In what ways are you a coworker with God? How is your work an extension of God's work? One example follows:

   - "God wants to see people fed. The packing cartons that my company produces are used quite extensively by a cereal manufacturer. So ultimately I'm helping in the job of feeding people."

9. How do you think God feels about what you do for a living? For example:

   - "God wants to promote health for people. As a nurse, I'm part of a system that provides health care to people. I think God is very pleased by that."

FOR FURTHER STUDY

Scripture
   - Psalm 111—Praises God for His work.
   - Ecclesiastes 3:12-13—Calls work a gift from God.
   - Colossians 3:23—Describes our participation with Christ in everyday work.

Reading

Bernbaum, John A. and Simon M. Steer. *Why Work?: Careers and Employment in Biblical Perspective.* Grand Rapids, Mich.: Baker Book House, 1986.

Henry, Carl F.H. *Aspects of Christian Social Ethics.* Grand Rapids, Mich.: Baker Book House, 1964.

Peabody, Larry. *Secular Work Is Full-Time Service.* Fort Washington, Pa.: Christian Literature Crusade, 1974.

Projects

1. Look through some magazines with your kids. Ask them to point out as many different kinds of work and occupations as they can. Remind them that such work is a gift from God.
2. At your next meal, begin by thanking God for the food. Then spend the rest of the meal listing all the occupations and people God used along the way to provide that food—farmers, truckdrivers, grocers, etc. (Your list should include no *less* than twenty-five people!)
3. Get a concordance and look up all the references in Scripture to God's "work."

GOD'S WORK—YOUR WORK

Everyday work fulfills at least five important purposes, according to the Bible:

1. Through work we serve people.
2. Through work we meet our own needs.
3. Through work we meet our family's needs.
4. Through work we earn money to give to others.
5. Through work we love God.

In this session we want you to evaluate how *your* work fulfills these purposes.

THROUGH WORK WE SERVE PEOPLE

Read the following scripture passage out loud.

> Let no debt remain outstanding, except the continuing debt to love one another, for he who loves his fellowman has fulfilled the law. The commandments, "Do not commit adultery," "Do not murder," "Do not steal," "Do not covet," and whatever other commandment there may be, are summed up in this one rule: "Love your neighbor as yourself." Love does no harm to its neighbor. Therefore love is the fulfillment of the law. (Romans 13:8-10, NIV)

Discussion

1. How does your work, and the products or services you help provide, meet the needs of people? (You may have to think quite broadly!) Some examples:

   • "As a teacher, my work helps children learn to read."
   • "I'm a computer programmer. The work that I do is used quite a bit by insurance companies to process claim forms. So because of my work, people are able to pay for health care or to provide for their families if they become disabled or die."
   • "I run an ad agency. Because of my work, my employees can earn a living to provide for their families."

THROUGH WORK WE MEET OUR OWN NEEDS AND THOSE OF OUR FAMILY

Make it your ambition to lead a quiet life, to mind your own business and to work with your hands, just as we told you, so that your daily life may win the respect of outsiders and so that you will not be dependent on anybody. (1 Thessalonians 4:11-12, NIV)

Discussion

2. List some ways your job provides for your basic needs.

3. a. If you are out of work, what is the reason?

   b. What action are you taking to provide for your family? (See chapter 10 in the book, *Finding a Job You Can Love.*)

THROUGH WORK WE EARN MONEY TO GIVE TO OTHERS

And let the one who is taught the word share all good things with him who teaches. (Galatians 6:6)

Let him who steals steal no longer; but rather let him labor, performing with his own hands what is good, in order that he may have something to share with him who has need. (Ephesians 4:28)

Discussion

4. Do you and your family have a written budget, and does that budget include giving money to the poor and to the support of Christian ministries?

5. In what ways might your skills and interests be made available free of charge to others who have needs? Some examples:

   • "As a teacher, I could tutor students twice a month."
   • "I'm a writer for a public relations firm. I could write a pamphlet or a brochure for an organization that works with the poor."
   • "I'm an electrician. If I could raise a small amount of money for travel, I could assist in a small construction project for a mission agency overseas."

6. Obviously none of us can or should take on the responsibility of meeting all the needs in the world. But what financial needs lie close at hand that you could help to meet?

   • Do you know someone who is destitute who could use food and shelter? How could you help him?
   • Do you know of an organization or an individual involved in some aspect of Christian ministry or missions that needs financial assistance? How can you help?

THROUGH WORK WE LOVE GOD

Whatever you do, do your work heartily, as for the Lord rather than for men. (Colossians 3:23)

"If you want to love God through your work, then you need to determine that what you are doing in your job is something God *wants* done, and that you are doing your job *because* God wants it done."[1]

Discussion

7. How about *your* work? Is your job something God wants done? Explain how it is, or why it isn't.

8. To what extent do you do your job because God wants you to do it?

FOR FURTHER STUDY

Scripture
- Leviticus 19:9-10—Gives an example of God's desire to see His people help provide for the poor.
- Psalm 15—Describes the intimate connection between our love for God and our work.
- Romans 13:8-10—Speaks of love as our highest obligation in every relationship.
- 2 Thessalonians 3:6-15—Exhorts us to work hard in order to provide for our own needs and those of our families.

Reading
Colson, Charles. *Loving God.* Grand Rapids, Mich.: Zondervan Publishing House, 1984. (Chapter 14, "The Everyday Business of Holiness," is very helpful.)

Projects
1. Do your children understand what you do for work, and how it serves people? If not, plan a time to discuss this with them. Better yet, invite them to go with you to your workplace sometime. When they see where you work, explain what you do and how it fits with the overall objectives of your employer. If possible, demonstrate the product or service you provide, and how it serves people.

2. Next time you make out checks for your giving, involve your spouse and/or children. Explain clearly why you are giving the money, and pray together as a family for those who will receive it.

3. Often our perspective on work as love for God and love for others gets clouded by the money we make. Obviously, it's not wrong to make money for honest labor or investment. But if you want to try working at a task purely for the sake of others, and totally apart from any remuneration, consider a short-term mission project.

   You have valuable God-given skills that could be extremely useful to people around the world. And many mission agencies have opportunities for brief, temporary involvement that will enable you to put those skills to work for others. Typical assignments last anywhere from two weeks to six months.

   For more information about this idea, and how to match your abilities with an appropriate opportunity, contact Intercristo at P.O. Box 33487, Seattle, WA 98133, 1-800-251-7740.

NOTE: 1. Doug Sherman and William Hendricks, *Your Work Matters to God* (Colorado Springs, Colo.: NavPress, 1987), page 93.

IT'S A JUNGLE OUT THERE!

It is not difficult to see the tragic consequences of sin on work. Even though work has inherent value to God, and even though we can use it to accomplish His purposes, we cannot escape the fact that we live and work in a fallen world, a world hostile to God.

In this session, we want you to examine the impact of sin on your own life and work.

SIN MAKES YOUR WORK HARDER

Read the following passage out loud.

> Then to Adam He said, "Because you have listened to the voice of your wife, and have eaten from the tree about which I commanded you, saying, 'You shall not eat from it';
> Cursed is the ground because of you;
> In toil you shall eat of it
> All the days of your life.
> Both thorns and thistles it shall grow for you;
> And you shall eat the plants of the field;
> By the sweat of your face
> You shall eat bread,
> Till you return to the ground,
> Because from it you were taken;
> For you are dust,
> And to dust you shall return." (Genesis 3:17-19)

Discussion

1. Imagine that you are doing your job *prior* to Genesis 3, that is, in the Garden of Eden. Describe what your job might look like in such a setting. Be creative!

2. Of course, you work after the Fall, in the midst of a sinful world. How is your particular job made more difficult as a result of sin in our world? How would it be easier if you didn't have to contend with sin?

SIN HAS MADE YOUR LIFE AND ITS WORK "FUTILE"

For the creation was subjected to frustration, not by its own choice, but by the will of the one who subjected it, in hope that the creation itself will be liberated from its bondage to decay and brought into the glorious freedom of the children of God.

We know that the whole creation has been groaning as in the pains of childbirth right up to the present time. (Romans 8:20-22, NIV)

The original word for *futile* does *not* mean absurd, meaningless, or without purpose. Rather, it means that life is transitory, passing, and therefore frustrating. If you try to base the significance and meaning of your life on the pursuits of life itself (including work), you'll find that significance and meaning are as transitory as life is. By contrast, if you base your life on God, who is outside the system, you can live in and accept this very transient, "futile" life with a moderate sense of satisfaction and joy.

Discussion

3. a. How do most people in your profession or occupation attempt to find meaning and value for their lives?

   b. Do they succeed in finding it? Why or why not?

4. If you were to die tonight, what aspects of your current job would live on and make a difference . . .

a year from now?

five years from now?

twenty-five or a hundred years from now?

SIN AFFECTS YOU, YOUR COWORKERS, AND THE SYSTEM

There is none righteous, not even one;
There is none who understands,
There is none who seeks for God;
All have turned aside, together they have become useless. . . .
For all have sinned and fall short of the glory of God.
(Romans 3:10-12,23)

Discussion

5. Describe an instance you know of in which people in your industry or profession compromised moral standards or displayed questionable ethics.

6. In what aspect of your occupation or profession do you most often see repeated, flagrant, and even accepted compromises of ethics and integrity?

7. a. Describe an instance in which you compromised your own Christian values on the job.

b. Why did you do it?

   c. What were the results?

8. Name one sin that you feel most tempted to commit on your
   job. (As a group, pray for each other, that God will help you
   avoid evil [James 5:16].)

FOR FURTHER STUDY

Scripture
   • Psalm 90—Describes the transitory nature of this life and
     how we should respond to an eternal God in light of it.
   • Ephesians 2:1-3—Describes the sinful condition of all of us.
   • 1 John 2:15-17—Exhorts us not to set our affections on a
     world corrupted by sin.

Reading
Lewis, C.S. *Mere Christianity*. ("Right and Wrong as a Clue to the
   Meaning of the Universe" is an excellent description of how
   sin has a stranglehold on the world.) New York: Macmillan,
   1964.

Projects
   1. On page 105 of *Your Work Matters to God* we describe some
      ways that sin can affect your actions, attitudes, and motives
      on the job. Take an inventory of your life and ask yourself,
      What sinful behaviors and thoughts do I bring to my job? List
      these on a sheet of paper, and then confess them as sin to
      God. You may also find it helpful to admit them to one other
      person who you trust and have confidence in.
   2. As a result of this discussion and/or your work on project 1,
      have you uncovered ways in which you need to make restitu-
      tion to someone? Do you need to pay back money you have
      gained unethically? Do you need to admit to someone that
      you lied? If so, go and do that right away.

NEW WORK OR NEW WORKERS?

If the last session seemed somewhat gloomy or depressing, this session should come as a welcome breath of fresh air! Christ's atoning work on the cross has dealt with your greatest enemy—sin.

In this session we want you to start applying this good news, and see how it makes a real difference for you as a worker!

CHRIST PUTS YOU IN RIGHT RELATIONSHIP WITH GOD

Therefore having been justified by faith, we have peace with God through our Lord Jesus Christ, through whom also we have obtained our introduction by faith into this grace in which we stand; and we exult in hope of the glory of God. (Romans 5:1-2)

Discussion

1. Christ's death has done everything necessary to reestablish a relationship between you and God. When and how did you enter into that relationship?

2. a. If you have not entered into a relationship with God, explain why not.

57

b. What would it take for you to do that?

CHRIST PUTS YOUR WORK BACK IN RIGHT RELATIONSHIP TO GOD

For we are His workmanship, created in Christ Jesus for good works, which God prepared beforehand, that we should walk in them. (Ephesians 2:10)

We tend to think of "good works" as acts of charity, mercy, and service. And those certainly are. But God also intends for our every-day work to be a "good work"—a work that brings honor to Him and accomplishes His purposes.

Discussion

3. Think about your job. Describe how it could bring honor to God and accomplish His purposes.

4. Read Colossians 3:22-24. How would your performance and attitude on the job be different if Jesus Christ met you *first thing tomorrow* when you arrive at work?

5. Evaluate yourself below in a quick inventory of your work-style. Grade yourself "A," "B," "C," "D," or "F," in each area.

	HIGH HONOR			FAILURE	
Your motive for going to work	A	B	C	D	F
Your use of time	A	B	C	D	F
Your relationship with your supervisor/partner(s)	A	B	C	D	F
Your relationships with your coworkers	A	B	C	D	F
Your relationships with your customers	A	B	C	D	F
Your relationships with your suppliers	A	B	C	D	F
Your use of your income	A	B	C	D	F

	HIGH HONOR			FAILURE	
Your honesty in filling out reports	A	B	C	D	F
Your follow-through on commitments	A	B	C	D	F
Your excellence in performing tasks	A	B	C	D	F
Your temper	A	B	C	D	F
Your language	A	B	C	D	F
Your testimony as a believer	A	B	C	D	F
Your courage to stand up to ethical compromise	A	B	C	D	F
Your sincerity of effort	A	B	C	D	F
Your ability to deal with conflict	A	B	C	D	F
Your reliability	A	B	C	D	F
Your competence	A	B	C	D	F
Your fairness in hiring	A	B	C	D	F
Your fairness in firing	A	B	C	D	F
Your use of emotional energy	A	B	C	D	F
Your responsibilities toward your spouse	A	B	C	D	F
Your responsibilities toward your children	A	B	C	D	F
Your management of debt	A	B	C	D	F
Your fairness in pricing	A	B	C	D	F
Your prayers regarding work issues	A	B	C	D	F
Your prayers for workplace decisions	A	B	C	D	F
Your attitude toward money	A	B	C	D	F

6. Look over your responses. How would Christ rate you in these same areas?

CHRIST WANTS TO TRANSFORM YOU AS A WORKER

You were taught, with regard to your former way of life, to put off your old self, which is being corrupted by its deceitful desires; to be made new in the attitude of your minds; and to put on the new self, created to be like God in true righteousness and holiness. (Ephesians 4:22-24, NIV)

Discussion

7. Which of your attitudes or behaviors that affect your work would you like to see Christ change or remove?

8. What attitudes or behaviors that affect your work would you like to see Christ build into you?

9. What active steps would *you* be willing to take to see these changes made?

FOR FURTHER STUDY

Scripture
- Romans 8:1-4,12-17—Describes the new relationship believers have with God.
- 2 Corinthians 5:17—Speaks of the newness of the believer who is in Christ.
- 1 Timothy 6:1—Describes the intimate connection between our work and the name or character of God.

Reading
Lewis, C.S. *Mere Christianity.* (Especially "Nice People or New Men.") New York: Macmillan, 1964.

Projects
1. Review the inventory of your workstyle. In what areas do you need to grow and make some corrections? Pick one of those areas and put it through the process for change described in session 13 of this study guide.

2. Write several paragraphs to describe the kind of worker you believe Christ wants you to be on your job. Then read through this description each day before you begin work.

WORKING FOR GOD

You may have noticed that we divided our book, *Your Work Matters to God,* into three parts. Part I talks about some of the problems that arise when we fail to see our work as God sees it. Part II presents the picture of work that the Bible paints—something that matters deeply to God. Part III deals with a few of the practical implications of this biblical view of work.

This session begins a study of Part III. In the discussion that follows, we want you to learn how to see *your* work as God's work, to learn how to do it His way, and to learn how to trust Him for the results.

HIS WORK: YOUR MOTIVES

Whatever you do, do your work heartily, as for the Lord rather than for men. (Colossians 3:23)

Discussion

1. Imagine that Jesus Christ were employed in the job you presently hold. Describe how He would approach your job.

   a. What would be His attitudes?

b. What motives would be important for Him to have?

c. How would this affect His behavior and performance?

2. What would have to change in your own attitudes and motives for you to approach your job as you think Christ would?

3. Pictured below is a business model that shows the three human roles involved in most work situations in our culture.

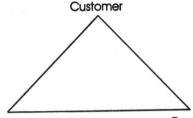

Customer

Employee or coworkers   Employer or boss

God's desire is that everyday work should help to meet the needs of *each* of these groups of people. That's why one of the purposes of work is *to serve people*.

a. *As an employee,* describe as many needs of your customers, your employer/boss, and your coworkers as you can think of, and how you can meet those needs.

b. *As an employer,* describe as many needs of your customers, your employees, and your coworkers as you can think of, and how your work can meet those needs.

4. Listed below are two sets of contrasting motives and attitudes. Look over these lists. Think carefully about how these items will affect the needs of the three groups of people in the business model, and how they will affect the work environment.

What Happens When . . . the employee
- cares only about his paycheck or commission?

- cheats or lies in order to shield the boss?

- undermines coworkers to get ahead?

the employer
- underpays his employees?

- fails to make a profit from the business?

- violates contracts, agreements, or standards?

the customer
- fails to pay for a product or service?

- withholds or falsifies required information in contracts and negotiations?

- doesn't fully explain his needs to the vendor?

What Happens When . . . the employee
- does his best to deliver the company's product or service?

- affirms and encourages coworkers?

- speaks up about safety or ethical violations?

the employer
- treats subordinates with respect and trust?

- ensures a safe and healthy work environment?

- fires a lazy, incompetent employee?

the customer
- educates himself about the product or service he needs?

- pays his bills on time?

- offers feedback on the goods or services he received?

HIS WAY: YOUR WORKSTYLE

Urge bondslaves to be subject to their own masters in everything, to be well-pleasing, not argumentative, not pilfering,
but showing all good faith that they may adorn the doctrine
of God our Savior in every respect. (Titus 2:9-10)

Discussion
This passage is one of many in the Bible that pictures a godly
"workstyle," that is, the *way* you do your work. Discuss the cate-
gories of this workstyle as follows.

5. *Authority:* Paul wanted workers "to be subject to their own
   masters in everything." Look carefully at your attitude and
   response to the authority structure of your job.

   a. How obediently do you carry out instructions and orders
      from your supervisor?

   b. How careful are you to obey laws, regulations, and stand-
      ards for your industry?

   c. At your job, in what ways do you subtly try to subvert or
      undermine the system?

6. *Excellence:* In Titus 2:9-10, Paul speaks of being "well pleas-
   ing." Think about to what extent you do your work in a pursuit of competence and excellence.

   a. If you're in a manufacturing or production role, do you
      take pains to ensure quality craftsmanship? If you're in a
      service or sales role, do you make every effort to supply
      value, and are you concerned with the needs of the
      customer?

b. Do you stay on top of new developments and technologies in your industry or profession?

c. Do you give your employer a full day's work for a full day's pay?

7. *Conflict:* This passage in Titus urges us to not be "argumentative." Evaluate your response to conflict on the job.

a. Are you known for being hostile and belligerent if things don't go your way, or are you able to discuss conflicts in a reasonable manner?

b. Do you avoid open conflict but get even through subtle, passive aggression, or do you engage in discussion of problems?

8. *Integrity:* Paul says that a godly workstyle means not pilfering. Think about what your own integrity is like on the job.

a. Do you steal time from your employer by taking too long for lunch, calling in sick when not sick, or just plain loafing?

b. Do you use company supplies for personal use, or make personal long-distance phone calls on company phones?

9. *Reliability:* This passage in Titus says that godly workers show "all good faith" in their work. This has to do with trustworthiness and reliability.

a. Are you known as a person who keeps his word?

b. Are you willing to honor commitments of time, money, or participation, even if it proves personally costly?

c. Can people depend on you to get the job done?

HIS RESULTS: YOUR OUTLOOK

Come now, you who say, "Today or tomorrow, we shall go to such and such a city, and spend a year there and engage in business and make a profit." Yet you do not know what your life will be like tomorrow. You are just a vapor that appears for a little while and then vanishes away. Instead, you ought to say, "If the Lord wills, we shall live and also do this or that." (James 4:13-15)

Discussion

10. At work you're paid to do a specific job that accomplishes certain purposes.

a. What are you supposed to accomplish through your job?

b. What are your expectations for the outcome of your efforts?

11. What factors that lie outside of your control could prevent you from accomplishing your objectives and fulfilling your expectations?

12. Is it hard for you to trust God for the things you can't control? Why or why not?

FOR FURTHER STUDY

Scripture

- Psalm 37—Contrasts the motives and workstyles of the righteous and the unrighteous.
- Proverbs 31:10-31—Records an outstanding description of the
  godly workstyle of a righteous woman.
- Jeremiah 17:7-8—Speaks of the blessing that comes from
  placing trust in God.

Reading

Peabody, Larry. *Secular Work Is Full-Time Service.* Fort Washing-
   ton, Pa.: Christian Literature Crusade, 1974.
White, Jerry and Mary White. *On the Job: Survival or Satisfaction.*
   Colorado Springs, Colo.: NavPress, 1988.

Projects

1. Write a career manifesto for how you're going to be distinctive
   for Christ in your job. (See pages 270-271 of our book.)

2. Using the business model shown on page 63, write a description of how you can bring a godly workstyle to your relationships with other employees, your employer, and your
   customers.

3. "In a decade's time, one-third of Americans experience at least
   one year in which their standard of living doubles. Thirty-one
   percent experience at least one year with a 50 percent drop in
   living standards."[1]
      Show this statistic to your spouse and then discuss the
   following questions: How would a substantial increase or
   decrease in our income affect our feelings about ourselves?
   Our marriage? Our values? Our attitudes toward God?

NOTE: 1. Greg J. Duncan, "On the Slippery Slope," *American Demographics* (Ithaca, N.Y.:
            American Demographics, Inc., May 1987), page 33.

FINDING A JOB YOU CAN LOVE

If your work matters deeply to God, then it makes sense that He has designed you to do certain kinds of work. Consequently, you should try to find a job that best utilizes that design. You should strive to make the greatest contribution you can to people in light of the resources and responsibilities God has given you.

In this session, we want you to evaluate whether you are making the best use of your God-given resources in your current vocation. This is not intended to be a complete career assessment. It is a chance for you to take stock of what you are doing with your life.

UNDERSTANDING YOUR DESIGN

Discussion

1. God has personally designed you and equipped you to accomplish certain tasks in this world. That design is not the only consideration for career decisions, but we feel it must be the starting point. Do you feel that you have a good understanding of that design? Review the following two lists in order to determine where you seem to fit.

The Person Who Doesn't Understand His Design	***The Person Who Understands His Design***
• often feels a lack of purpose in his work.	• feels great purpose and significance in his work.

- may change jobs fre-
quently.

- may feel chronically bored
at work.

- is confused about where
his career is headed.

- tends toward chronic "burn
out."

- often works hard at things
he's not very good at.

- finds that many of his skills
lie unused, underused, or
misused on the job.

- frequently takes on tasks
that only frustrate him.

- faces excessive conflict and
frustration with coworkers,
bosses, and "the system."

- thinks more about the
work he'd "like" to do than
what he's been given to do.

- works well at a job until
and unless it is time to
change jobs.

- is stimulated regularly by
work opportunities and
assignments.

- has confidence and direction about what he's cut out
to do, no matter where his
job path takes him.

- enjoys a sense of pacing
and an understanding of his
capabilities and limits.

- works hard at things he
knows he will do well and
deemphasizes things he's not
good at.

- uses the majority of his
skills regularly to accomplish
tasks.

- knows what opportunities
to decline.

- understands how best to
work and relate to others on
the job.

- chooses job opportunities
that make the best use of his
design.

You may have discovered that you really *don't* understand
your design by God. You may find that many or most of the

statements on the left above apply to you. *If so, you need
some form of personal assessment.* The best resource we can
recommend to help you get started is a paperback by Ralph
Mattson and Art Miller called *Finding a Job You Can Love.*
You should be able to get a copy at a Christian bookstore. If
you're not sure that you clearly understand your design, *you
need to read that book and go through the exercises in it!*

2. Knowing your design, of course, doesn't ensure that you are
using that design in a responsible way. A person can use his
or her God-given resources for selfish purposes, rather than to
serve God and meet the needs of people. To what extent does
your current job serve God and the legitimate needs of
people?

3. By now you may be thinking about whether you should
change jobs! If you are, explain why you feel a change might
be in order. Consider these questions:

- Do I want to change jobs primarily because there is not a
good match between my God-given design and the responsibilities and tasks of my present job?
- Do I have something that I'm moving toward, or am I
merely running from a difficult situation?
- How could I stay in the job and make it more workable?
- Am I being tempted to leave a job that basically fits who I
am merely by offers of a higher salary, better location, more
prestige, or some other secondary consideration?

Your God-given design is not the only consideration for career
decisions. Things like financial needs, family needs and responsibilities, experience, and education also enter in. For an excellent
and comprehensive resource in career direction, you should obtain
the "Career Kit" from Intercristo, 1-800-251-7740.

FOR FURTHER STUDY

Scripture
- Psalm 139—Describes the intimate care and concern with which God has crafted you.
- Hebrews 11—Lists the heroes of faith from the Old Testament. Notice how many different occupations there are!

Reading

Bowles. *What Color Is Your Parachute?* Berkeley, Calif.: Ten Speed Press, 1977.

Friesen, Gary. *Decision Making and the Will of God.* Portland, Oreg.: Multnomah Press, 1980.

Germann, Richard and Peter Arnold. *Job and Career Building.* Berkeley, Calif.: Ten Speed Press, 1980.

Mattson, Ralph and Arthur Miller. *Finding a Job You Can Love.* Nashville, Tenn.: Thomas Nelson Publishers, 1982.

Projects

1. Even if you don't feel you need full-blown career counseling, you would still benefit enormously from Mattson and Miller's patented process of assessment, called "The System for Identifying Motivated Abilities" (SIMA). *We can't urge you enough to go through it*—even if you've been through other kinds of career assessment.

   Depending on your needs, level of interest, and level of occupation, you have three options to consider:

   - You can read Mattson and Miller's book, *Finding a Job You Can Love,* which explains the process and has some assessment exercises.
   - You can order the "Career Kit," mentioned earlier from Intercristo, which includes an authorized version of the SIMA assessment tool.
   - You can contact People Management, Inc. (10 Station Street, Simsbury, CT 06070, 203-651-3581) about their specialized assessment programs and other consulting services.

2. Help your children get started early on knowing and appreciating their design from God. Select one or two accomplish-

ments that each child enjoys doing and feels he or she does well, and ask, "What is it about that accomplishment that you enjoy so much?" Their answers may give you real insight into what motivates them.

WHAT CAN ONE PERSON DO?

Dealing with evil in the workplace is a complex problem. We live and work in a world infected by sin. We see that sin every day—in major corporations, in branches of government and other institutions, in individuals with whom we work, and in our own lives as well.

Confronted with evil all around us and in us, it's easy to throw up our hands in despair. "What can one person do?" we ask. And yet, because God takes us and our work very seriously, and because He wants to make us like Christ, He expects us to face sin squarely, and do what we can to "overcome evil with good" (Romans 12:21).

In this session we want you to determine how *you* can "overcome evil with good" where you work. You'll examine an actual situation you face on the job, decide whether you should act, and why, and what you should do.

YOUR SITUATION

No matter where you work or what you do, you run into situations where some evil exists and exerts its influence. Describe some evil you see in your *work* environment.

Discussion

1. Explain your work circumstances generally, and then explain what about the situation you believe is wrong. For example:

●You may be a sales rep whose boss has instructed you to lie in order to close a deal.

●You may be a secretary whose boss has accepted a bribe or kickback.

●You may be a military officer who knows of a political "hatchet job" being carried out to get rid of another officer.

SHOULD YOU ACT?

There are at least four circumstances that should trigger some response from you as a Christian:

●You must act if you are asked to do what is wrong.

●You should act when your own conscience is violated.

●You should act when it is in your power to end or avoid evil.

●You should act when innocent people stand to be affected by evil.

Discussion
2. a. Which of these circumstances matches your situation? (If you are unsure about any of the four circumstances mentioned, you may want to review pages 154-157 in *Your Work Matters to God.*)

   b. Do you believe you need to act? Why or why not?

WHAT SHOULD YOU DO?

We make a number of suggestions in the book as to how you can confront evil in your workplace. No doubt you can think of other ideas.

3. Go through the following list of questions to see how you might develop a personal strategy to deal with your situation.

a. In your view, who is most responsible for causing the evil you see? Is there any way to confront this person(s)?

b. Who is in the best position to do something about the problem? Can you discuss it with him or her?

c. God has given you abilities, a personality, resources, relationships, position, and other means of leverage and influence. In light of these resources, how do *you* feel you could be most effective in dealing with this situation?

d. As you think about your situation and how it might be changed, what do you think is realistic? What limited, measurable gains could be accomplished? What creative options can you think of?

e. What negative consequences should you anticipate as you begin to act in this situation? Have you counted the cost and the risks? Are those risks worth taking? Are you willing and prepared to take them?

f. Is it possible that you need to leave the situation? Are you willing to endure a hostile environment if necessary? Are you willing to sacrifice personal comfort, convenience, and job security to maintain your personal integrity?

g. Describe the extent to which you are praying about this situation. Have you allied yourself with other believers who will join you in prayer? What, exactly, are you asking God to do?

h. Are there aspects of your own character that are contributing evil to this situation? Are you pursuing personal purity as you confront the problem? Is there sin that you need to confess and deal with? Is there restitution that you need to make?

WHAT SHOULD YOU DO—STARTING NOW?

4. Write down the initial steps you plan to take *right away* to deal with your situation. Be specific! Some examples:

● "At the staff meeting tomorrow, I plan to ask John to see me afterwards. Then I plan to tell him that as his boss, I cannot condone what he is doing."

● "I plan to meet with Arlene, who is another Christian, for lunch once a week for a month. Neither of us has much influence in the situation, but we intend to pray about it each time we meet, and ask God to raise up someone who can deal with it."

FOR FURTHER STUDY

Scripture
● Daniel 6:1-5—The amazing testimony of Daniel, a government bureaucrat, who maintained his integrity in an incredibly evil empire.
● 1 Peter 3:13-17—Peter's exhortation to remain pure no matter what others around us are doing.

Reading
Sproul, R.C. *Stronger Than Steel: The Wayne Alderson Story.* San Francisco, Calif.: Harper & Row, 1950.

Lewis, C.S. *The Problem of Pain.* New York: Macmillan Co., 1943.

Projects

1. If you have compromised your integrity in a specific situation and need to make restitution, go and do that right away.

2. You may be struggling with problems of your own, let alone problems in your company. For instance, you may be ensnared by any of a number of addictions: alcohol, drugs, sex, gambling, eating, smoking, shopping sprees, work, lying, etc. If so, you need to contact a hotline or other resource in your area to find some help. In matters like these, the *worst* thing you can do is to deny there is a problem or think you are still in control. You're not. Your addiction controls you. You must get help.

THE PROBLEM OF GAIN

If your work matters to God, then the money you make from your work matters to God as well. After all, in today's world, money represents the "fruit" or reward of your labor. God cares deeply about how you handle those resources.

In this session, we want to help you evaluate your own income and lifestyle. You'll discuss three areas: what your overall attitude is toward material things; what you spend on yourself; and what you give away to others. Be prepared for an emotionally challenging discussion! The issue of lifestyle is one in which many tensions intersect, and there are no simple answers!

CONTENTMENT OR COVETOUSNESS?

1. a. Make a written list of fifteen to twenty items that you believe are absolutely essential expenses for you and your family. (Be prepared to explain why you have selected the items you have.) These may be tangible goods, such as certain food items or a certain level of housing, or intangible services, such as a certain type of education for your children, or a certain amount of life insurance.

   Be as specific as you'd like. Apart from anyone else, *you* determine what is "essential" for this list, what kinds of things are "musts" in order for you to live and function realistically in your culture. If you want, put down the cost per month of each of these items.

b. Place a check by the items that you already or normally have on a regular basis. Place a star or an asterisk by the items you don't have.

c. Now look at the items you have starred, the items you don't have. How does not having these things make you feel about yourself? About God? About the items themselves?

d. Next, look over the items you have checked, the items you already have. How does having these things make you feel about yourself? About God? About the items themselves?

Let your character be free from the love of money, being content with what you have; for He Himself has said, "I will never desert you, nor will I ever forsake you." (Hebrews 13:5)

Discussion
2. a. Describe your attitude toward your present lifestyle and material possessions.

b. Do you rest in the conviction that God intends to meet your needs? Why or why not?

LIMITS OR LUXURIES?

You've made a list of "absolutely essential" items, as you perceive them. In a sense, you have expressed what to you is the baseline of your lifestyle, the lower limits of what you feel it takes to live and function in this economy. (Note: This is *your* idea of the basics—not someone else's, not even God's.)

If you're like the majority of people using this discussion guide, most if not all of what you consider to be the basics are supplied by your income. In other words, you can get by on what you have.

3. a. Of course, then we start looking up the scale to things we don't have but would like to have—nonessentials and luxuries. Having listed the basics, now write a list of about twenty luxuries. (Be prepared to explain why you have selected the items you have.) List things that you don't presently have but think that someday you'll "need" or definitely expect to have—perhaps the ability to pay for a college education for your children, or a second home in the country. Also list the things you dream of owning, though it's doubtful whether you'll ever have them—maybe a certain car, or a ski chalet right on the slopes in Colorado, or a private plane. This time, feel free to sound extravagant! You may put a cost down, though with many items, as they say, "If you have to ask, you can't afford it!"

b. Place a check by the items that, while not absolutely essential, are nevertheless truly important and that you someday believe you should have. Place a star or an asterisk by the others, which are, by process of elimination, extravagancies and unnecessary luxuries.

c. Now comes the hard part! There's no escaping the fact that the Bible teaches us that as Christians our lives should be marked in some measure by the principles of sacrifice and discipline:

> Then Jesus said to His disciples, "If anyone wishes to come after Me, let him deny himself, and take up his cross, and follow Me. For whoever wishes to save his life shall lose it; but whoever loses his life for My sake shall find it. For what will a man be profited, if he gains the whole world, and forfeits his soul? Or what will a man give in exchange for his soul?" (Matthew 16:24-26)

Earlier you listed "absolute essentials." Then you divided nonessentials into important wants and unnecessary luxuries. In light of Matthew 16, would you be willing to draw the line at unnecessary luxuries? Would you be willing to live a *limited lifestyle*? If your income were to rise to the place where you could afford the important wants, would you be willing to stop there, and instead of buying unnecessary luxuries, invest that money in something outside yourself?

GENEROSITY OR GREED?

The Lord directed those who proclaim the gospel to get their living from the gospel. (1 Corinthians 9:14)

But whoever has the world's goods, and beholds his brother in need and closes his heart against him, how does the love of God abide in him? Little children, let us not love with word or with tongue, but in deed and truth. (1 John 3:17-18)

Discussion
4. Do you have a personal and/or family budget, and does that budget include giving to the poor and to Christian efforts?

5. In light of this entire session, how would you rate yourself on a scale of 1-5, "1" being "thoroughly greedy" and "5" being "thoroughly generous"? Explain your choice.

6. What one positive step do you think you need to take right away in the area of income and lifestyle?

FOR FURTHER STUDY

Scripture
- Proverbs 30:7-9—A prayer for material and spiritual balance.
- Matthew 6:25-34—Jesus' classic exhortation to us to put our trust in God's provision.

• 2 Corinthians 8:1-5—The astounding generosity of the Macedonian Christians.

Projects

1. If you do not have a personal and/or family budget, sit down (with your spouse if appropriate) and design one. Keep in mind the principles mentioned in our book: limited lifestyle, functional economy, generosity, etc.

2. If you do have a budget, review it (with your spouse), keeping in mind the same principles mentioned in project 1.

3. If you own or run a business, consider giving a certain portion of the profits to those with financial needs.

LIVING FOR THE WEEKEND

One of the greatest needs of Christians in our day is to learn how to put work in its proper perspective with the rest of life. This isn't just a need for better time management, though that certainly helps. Rather, it's a need to see that work is only one part of life, and that God desires to see us live for Him in every area.

In this session we want to help you get started on a strategy for growth in areas beyond work.

THE PENTATHLON

The New Testament shows us five major areas of life:

- Your personal life
- Your family
- Your church life
- Your work
- Your community

These are much like a pentathlon of five very diverse athletic events. In a pentathlon, you must train for and compete in all five events. You cannot excel in one area to the neglect of other areas, or you will lose the overall contest

Likewise, God desires that you honor Him in all five of the major areas mentioned. While work tends to take up more of your time and emotional energy than the other areas, you cannot

87

neglect the others without seriously compromising your overall responsibilities before God. In other words, you must learn to keep work in its proper perspective. You must learn to balance work with the other areas.

KEEP WORK IN ITS PROPER PERSPECTIVE

Obviously we can't completely reorganize your life and your schedule in one easy lesson! Your life, your habits, and your will are far too complex for change to happen quickly, permanently, and easily. But you can begin to take some small steps toward balancing work with other areas. In the exercise that follows, *you* will have a chance to decide what steps *you* want to take, and design a personalized strategy to take them.

Take a Personal Inventory
Begin by evaluating yourself in each of the five areas of the pentathlon. We've listed a few questions to help you get started. (Hundreds of other questions could be asked.) They all flow out of scriptural principles that instruct us in how to live our lives.

1. As you think through each area, the important question to ask yourself is, "What is *one way* in which I need to change, grow, and improve in this area?" Pray about each area, asking God how *He* wants to change you, then name the one way you need to improve in that area.

   a. In your *personal life,* what is the status of the disciplines that result in spiritual growth, activities such as Scripture reading and study, Scripture memory, prayer, and the reading of devotional literature? What about your physical condition and habits of eating, exercise, sleep, and relaxation? What behaviors do you especially desire to overcome? What behaviors do you especially desire to establish?

   b. In your *family life,* do you have a set come-home time that your family can count on? Do you "date" your spouse regularly? Do you disengage emotionally from work in order to spend undistracted time with your children? Are you upholding your responsibilities to your parents, to your spouse's parents, and to other relatives?

c. In your *church life,* how often do you place yourself under the instruction of Scripture? Do you faithfully, generously, and joyfully donate money to the cause of Christ? Are you praying regularly for your pastor and other church leaders? Do you know what your spiritual gifts are, and are you using them?

d. In your *work,* do you give an honest day's labor to your employer? Do you follow through on commitments you make to your customers? Are you informed about new developments, ideas, methods, and people in your field? To the extent that you can, do you hold a steady job by which your needs and those of your family are being adequately met? Do you have a family budget, and do you live within it?

e. In your *community,* do you regularly exercise your right and responsibility as a United States citizen to cast an informed vote? Do you pay your fair share of taxes? What is the status of your driving record? Do you maintain your property within the statutes of your community? Are you conscious of and involved with the poor and their needs?

Plan Your Steps

You have now evaluated yourself and come up with five ways you'd like to see growth—one for each of the five areas of the pentathlon. Now it's time to plan some steps toward making that growth happen.

2. You may not have enough time to plan steps for all five areas, so for now, pick *one* area. (You can go through this process for the other four areas later.)

a. What is one simple thing you could do to get moving toward growth and change? Ask God for insight, and then write out your answer. For example:

• In my family life, I need to spend more time with my son, so I'll plan to play basketball with him this week.

b. If you're like most of us, what you've written down so far is a good start, but far from a well-planned action step. You need to revise your goal to make it:

• *Simple:* Is it a single, complete action or activity? Or is it too complicated, with too many steps?
• *Measurable:* Can you definitely say whether or not you have taken the step? Or is it so general and intangible that you'll never know whether you've done it?
• *Achievable:* Is it something realistic and "do-able"? Or is it so lofty or unrealistic that you'd have to be superman or superwoman to pull it off?
• *Compatible:* Is it compatible with your other commitments? Or are you simply adding more to your schedule than you can possibly handle?

Evaluate the action step you wrote for question 1 according to these four criteria and revise it. For example:

• I need to spend more time with my son. I'll plan to play basketball with him Thursday afternoon at 5:15 and Saturday morning at 11:00.

Discuss your revised answer with someone and let him evaluate how well it fits with the four criteria mentioned. (This is a good group activity.) The point is not to pick apart your goal, but to help you design a step that you will *actively* take toward growth!

c. One more thing: Write down any preliminary steps that you need to add in order to make your goal happen. For example:

If I'm going to play basketball with my son this week, I'll need to . . .
- check with him to make sure he's available.
- get new laces for my athletic shoes.
- tell my secretary not to schedule anything past 4:30 on Thursday.

HOLD YOURSELF ACCOUNTABLE

Good intentions are worthless apart from action. Good plans are *only* plans and good intentions unless they *degenerate* into work.

How can that happen? Perhaps you're the one person in a million who has loads of initiative and self-discipline. The rest of us need help when it comes to ensuring follow-through. Only we can accomplish our goals. But knowing that others stand with us, who are concerned for our growth toward Christlikeness, can be a big help.

3. Write down the names of one or two people with whom you will share your action step. Ask them to check to see whether you've accomplished it.

MEASURE YOUR PROGRESS

4. Having gone to this much trouble to set up a small plan for growth, you should also include a way to measure—and celebrate—your progress. In a way, holding yourself accountable to someone will accomplish that; but two other steps will help as well.

a. Pull out your calendar or schedule book and *write down* the specific times or days when you plan to accomplish your action step.

b. Write your action step in the following checklist. Once you
   go through this entire process for the other four areas of
   the pentathlon, you can record the other action steps in it
   as well. Then, once a week or so, you can review the checklist and measure your progress.

A Personal Checklist for Growth

CATEGORY	ACTION STEP	DATES, TIMES	ENTERED INTO SCHEDULE	COMPLETED
Family Example	*Play basket- ball with son.*	*Thurs., 5:00 Sat., 11:00*		
Personal				
Family				
Work				
Church				
Community				

ONE WORD OF CAUTION

We've tried to offer you a strategy for learning to please God in the
various areas of your life. However, nothing could be worse than to
think, "If I just do these steps, then I'll please God!" This is a very
subtle error that has plagued followers of God ever since He began
to reveal His will to mankind. This is the error of legalism.

The legalist takes the view that "God accepts me because of
what I'm doing." The person who believes this is out to "prove"
that he is worthy of or that he deserves God's love. In essence, he
sets up a sort of "deal" with God: "God has laid down a certain
code. Therefore, if I live according to that code, I will please Him.
And if I please Him, then He is obligated to love me, for I will have

satisfied His code."

It all sounds airtight! Too bad that it will inevitably end in wretchedness—the wretchedness of trying to live up to ever-higher, impossibly demanding standards; of comparing oneself to others, resulting in either self-condemnation, or in pride and the condemnation of another; of living with guilt, constantly weighted down with a sense of God's displeasure; and being consumed with rage because God has not lived up to His end of the "bargain."

To avoid such a fate, we urge you to keep these perspectives in mind:

- God never accepts you because of what *you* do, but because of what *He* has done for you in Christ. God "owes" you *nothing!* He never has and never will—no matter *what* you do! The *basis* of our relationship with God—which is really the heart of the matter for the legalist—is God's *grace*. When there was nothing we could do to regain a relationship with God, He did *everything* that was necessary to re-establish that possibility.

- As for obedience to God's moral code, it is vitally important—but not as a *basis* for our relationship with God. It is just at this point that the legalist confuses the *means* with the *end.* The legalist believes that his adherence to standards secures God's favor, and therefore is what matters ultimately. Right conduct becomes an end in itself.

  But God has already shown His grace to be the basis for our relationship with Him. Far from trying to "prove" our love for God or our worthiness to receive His love, we should accept His acceptance of us and respond in *gratitude.* We should seek to please God—not to *establish* our life with Him, *because* He has established it in Christ.

- Obedience to Christ is vitally important, because in obeying Him we become like Him. And Christlikeness is the goal of the Christian life. God brings us back into right relation with Himself in order to make us into a certain kind of people: people of high moral character, of courage, of joy, of freedom, of faith, of health. People, in short, who through their unique personalities display the character of Christ.

• In this session, we have suggested a strategy for you to use in becoming like Christ. Many have found this strategy to be helpful in their growth. But you may not! Checklists and inventories and accountability groups may not fit your personality or your "style." That's fine. Use other approaches if they help you more. But by all means, pursue Christ, and pursue a character that pleases Him!

FOR FURTHER STUDY

Scripture
- Psalm 127—A psalm that puts work in its proper perspective with the rest of life.
- Proverbs 8:22-31—Describes the delight, the joy, and the play that God enjoys in His work of creation.
- Ecclesiastes 3:1-8—The classic passage that reminds us that life is full of many experiences—only some of which relate to work.
- Ephesians 5:15-16—Paul's exhortation to us to make wise use of our time.

Reading
Hansel, Tim. *When I Relax, I Feel Guilty.* Elgin, Ill.: David C. Cook, 1979.

MacDonald, Gordon. *Restoring Your Spiritual Passion.* Nashville: Thomas Nelson, Inc., 1986.

Projects
1. If your life is completely out of control and mismanaged, you probably need to walk away from it for at least two weeks, longer if possible, to "dry out." You need rest, distance, and time just to gain some perspective and give yourself a chance to think clearly.

   But that's just a start. You then need to ask yourself some hard questions.

   a. Why are you driven to work so hard and so long? Is it a healthy or unhealthy drive?

b. Are you sacrificing your marriage and/or family in order to reach your career goals? Biblically, that's too high a price to pay.

c. What is the quality of your relationship to Christ? Is He free to do with you and your career whatever He desires? Or is He merely the caboose on a train driven by your career success?

d. Are you making the wisest use of your God-given design in your work (see session 10)? Are you trying to do that for which you have not fundamentally been equipped by God?

Hard questions are valuable, but sooner or later they must degenerate into tough choices and *action*:

e. What changes must you make—in your attitudes, your schedule, your commitments, your work—in order to put work in its proper perspective?

f. What limits will you set and honor in regard to work? Limits take courage and faith!

g. What people can help you make the necessary changes toward a biblical, healthy life? Your spouse? Your secretary? Your boss? Your business partner? In what specific way could each one help?

2. As a family, sit down together and discuss your weekly schedule in light of the five areas of the pentathlon. Be realistic about the commitments everyone makes!

3. If you're single, it's especially easy for work to consume your life. But the five areas of the pentathlon apply to you as well. One of the healthiest things you could do to gain perspective on your work is a short-term missions project. See page 51 for more information about this.

THE NEW CLERGY

Your work matters to God. How much does it matter? Just as much as the work of any pastor, any preacher, any missionary, or anyone else in "full-time" vocational Christian ministry.

This truth has *profound* implications! For one thing, it means that you don't have to quit your job and go into the ministry to serve God. You can and should serve Him "full-time" in your present job. Furthermore, you don't have to do "church work" to serve God. While your church is important and provides one setting in which to serve God, you can and should also serve Him *outside* your church. In this session, we want to help you start setting your sights on how you can do God's work outside your church.

But first, a qualifier: We *in no way* want to undermine your commitment and loyalty to your church and its leaders. In fact, if you're not a part of a local congregation of believers, you need to find such a group and commit yourself to it. You need a church to help you worship, to help you learn about God and His Word, to build relationships with other Christians, as a place to serve other believers, and for many other reasons. However, most of us also need to look outside our churches for opportunities to serve God. That's what the following discussion is all about.

WHERE SHOULD *YOU* SERVE?

A pastor at a large denominational church in a major metropolitan area once told his congregation,

According to a study which I read several years ago, no church can create enough meaningful jobs for all of its members to do something in church. In fact, only one-third of the membership of a local church can be given a job doing church work. So if you think that serving the Lord means doing some work in church, then two-thirds of you are doomed to frustration and disappointment.[1]

Discussion

1. Do you see yourself as part of the one-third involved in church work, or as part of the two-thirds who must look outside of your church for service opportunities?

2. Do you sometimes feel frustrated that your abilities and motivations for serving God don't seem to find much opportunity for expression through the programs of your church? Or do you easily and eagerly find ways to serve at church?

3. No doubt your church has *many* opportunities for service. And no doubt many of those opportunities go unfilled. If few or none of these church service opportunities seem like something you'd choose to do, why is that the case? On the other hand, if these kinds of opportunities tend to be the *primary* way you express your service, why is that the case?

4. Based on the previous discussion, will you most likely express your service to God in and through the programs of your church, almost totally outside the programs of your church, or somehow in both contexts?

HOW WILL YOU SERVE?

You as a layperson are part of a "new clergy," and as such, you need to do the work of God wherever it needs doing. The Apostle Paul exhorts us that *whatever* we do, we should do it with a view toward serving Christ (Colossians 3:17). But that's a general principle for life. Let's get much more specific about how you uniquely serve Christ and serve the needs of people. To do that, you'll need to do a good bit of self-evaluation. If you're going to be a tool in God's hand, it's rather important that you have at least some idea what kind of tool you are!

Listed here are some questions we typically ask someone who needs direction in this regard. Others could be added, but these are a start. Spend as much time as you'd like on your answers. The more data you provide, the better you'll be able to determine areas of service.

The point of this exercise is to help you gain a sense of confidence that God has given you a way to serve Him meaningfully.

Discussion

5. a. How would you describe your overall bent in life? What motivates you? For example:

   - "When I see someone in need, I just have to help them."
   - "I'm a tremendously competitive person. I live for winning, no matter what the game is."
   - "I'm an adventurer. I'm always either traveling or doing some high-risk thing like hang gliding."

   b. Describe your personality.

   c. Describe your work. Include the nature and scope of your responsibilities, the ways in which you find it most satisfying and also least satisfying, the nature of your relationships to others on the job, career highlights, etc.

   d. As you think about the needs of people and the broad needs of society, what things tear at your heart? As a friend of ours, Bobb Biehl, asks, "What things make you weep or pound the table?"

e. Which of the needs you just listed do you think you could do something about? Why? What would you like to do?

f. In what way do you think you could make your greatest contribution to God's work in the world? To what extent does your current job match that contribution?

g. If in answering question f above you determine that your greatest contribution will probably occur primarily outside of your work, where will you likely make that contribution?

h. Evaluate your answers to questions e-g in light of your time, your many responsibilities, and your financial situation. What is realistic for you right now?

i. As best you can, describe specifically how and where you intend to express your service to God.

j. What would others who know you well say about your answer to question i? Whose suggestions and helpful insights could you benefit from?

FOR FURTHER STUDY

Scripture
- Romans 16—Read through this list of people to see how many others besides Paul were accomplishing "God's work" in Rome.

• Ephesians 4:11-13—The classic text on the nature and function of the church.

Projects

1. You may not belong to a local church, or you may be dissatisfied with the teaching and/or worship of the church you currently attend. In either case, it's *imperative* that you find some group of Christians with whom you can study God's Word, worship Him, and encourage and support each other. You'll never find a perfect church, but seek out a fellowship that is at least growing in the right direction.

2. If you have not gone through the personal assessment described in session 10, do so now! If you have gone through it, use the self-knowledge you've gained to determine where you could best serve God.

NOTE: 1. Dr. Clayton Bell, sermon preached at Highland Park Presbyterian Church, Dallas, Texas, September 22, 1985.

EVERY CHRISTIAN A LEADER!

In session 14 we tried to encourage you to look for opportunities to serve God not only in and through your church, but in your workplace and in the world at large as well. When you do that, you immediately notice how many people around you have no relationship with God. But they do have a relationship with you!

In this session we want you to think strategically about how you can influence these nonChristians for Christ. We want you to become a *leader* for God where you work.

WHO IS A LEADER?

Read the following scripture passages:

> You are the light of the world. A city set on a hill cannot be hidden. . . . Let your light shine before men in such a way that they may see your good works, and glorify your Father who is in heaven. (Matthew 5:14,16)

> Be imitators of me, just as I also am of Christ. (1 Corinthians 11:1)

> But even if I am being poured out as a drink offering upon the sacrifice and service of your faith, I rejoice and share my joy with you all. (Philippians 2:17)

> The things you have learned and received and heard and seen in me, practice these things; and the God of peace shall be with you. (Philippians 4:9)

> For our gospel did not come to you in word only, but also in power and in the Holy Spirit and with full conviction; just as you know what kind of men we proved to be among you for your sake. You also became imitators of us and of the Lord, having received the word in much tribulation with the joy of the Holy Spirit, so that you became an example to all the believers in Macedonia and in Achaia. (1 Thessalonians 1:5-7)

Douglas Hyde, former leader in the Communist party in England, wrote the following in *Dedication and Leadership*:

> The task of making leaders is really one of creating an attitude of mind. When some new situation arises, the reaction of most people is to ask: when is someone going to do something about it? The spontaneous reaction of the trained leader is at once to ask himself: what do I do in this situation?
>
> He comes before his fellows and says: We should do this and that and the other. And they follow him. Partly because he speaks with authority, they respect him and look up to him, but also because they have learned from experience that he has something to offer. . . .
>
> The Christian . . . might profitably ask: What do I do as a Christian? Then act accordingly. Something in the nature of a social revolution and a moral regeneration would occur in the life of the West if every committed Christian we already have were to acquire, or to be given, this attitude of mind and start to think in these terms.[1]

Discussion

1. The type of leadership presented by Hyde has nothing to do with the power of position or official rank and status. Yet it exerts a powerful *influence* on others.

   a. What makes a person a "leader"?

b. What gives him or her such influence?

2. Who do you follow? Why?

3. Hyde believes that profound cultural change would occur if Christians became leaders where they live and work. Do you agree? How does this relate to what Paul and Jesus say in the preceeding verses?

4. A friend of ours, Fred Smith Sr., says that the definition of a leader is "someone that others are following." Do people follow you? Why or why not?

ARE YOU A LEADER?

That you may prove yourselves to be blameless and innocent, children of God above reproach in the midst of a crooked and perverse generation, among whom you appear as lights in the world. (Philippians 2:15)

Douglas Hyde also writes:

The purpose of Christian leadership training is not just to help ambitious men to the top, or to make little men who have done leadership courses feel bigger than they really are. Still less is it to produce fuhrers, either large or small.

It has much more to do with the making of integrated people. Ones who understand what they believe, are deeply dedicated to it, and who try unceasingly to relate their beliefs to every facet of their own lives and to the society in which they live.[2]

Discussion
5. How would you describe your understanding of the basic truths of Christ, and the importance of those truths?

6. What difference do Christ and His truths make for your day-to-day life? How would your life be different if you did *not* know Him?

7. a. Are you willing to relate your beliefs to every facet of your own life—including your work—and to the society in which you live? Are you willing to "shine like a star" for Christ, as Paul says? It's easy to answer yes to these questions. But suppose it means losing your job, risking an investment, losing a friend, or inviting hostility?

   b. Are you an influencer or are you influenced by the surrounding culture? In other words, are you a leader or a follower?

WANTED: LEADERS FOR CHRIST

As a Christ-follower, you must become a leader for Christian thinking and influence in your workplace.[3]

The work world is not a neutral setting. You will either set the pace by living a distinctive Christlike lifestyle, or you will follow along with the mainstream. God has placed you among many people who have no relationship with Him. Your job is to do the best you can to encourage people toward God. Some will move toward Him, others away from Him. Your influence happens indirectly through your lifestyle and workstyle on the job, but it also can happen more directly.

Discussion

8. Write a list of as many nonChristians as you can think of with whom you have some relationship on the job. Include coworkers, superiors, subordinates, customers, vendors, even competitors. Depending on your occupation or position, you may have hundreds, even thousands, of people in your network! List your closer associates. (If this seems mechanical, it is! But you do this all day in your mind anyway, so writing names down shouldn't be a problem!)

9. Using the preceding list, describe . . .

    a. some of the people with whom you already have considerable influence.

    b. some with whom you have little or no influence.

    c. some with whom you would like to have some influence.

10. We won't ask you to pick out specific names to "target" for sharing the gospel. While this occasionally has some advantage, we find that it usually is more a hindrance than a help.

    Instead, we simply ask you to do this: As you review the individual names on your list, ask yourself, "Is there anything I can do right now that would influence this person toward God?" For example:

    ● "This person is new to the company and knows no one. I'll ask her to lunch to make her feel welcome."
    ● "This person is a close friend and has just lost a loved one. I'll make it a point to just be there for him, and to be available to take care of little details for him and his family."
    ● "This person is really confused about religion. I'll offer him a book, and then later we can discuss it together."

    Begin to brainstorm on paper *your own* strategies for influence.

11. Here are two obvious additional steps to your brainstorming:

    ● As you review your list, *pray* for each person. God may well impress upon you an opportunity for influence.

- Review the list regularly, perhaps once a week or so. You may even want to incorporate this into the checklist described in session 13 on page 92.

FOR FURTHER STUDY

Scripture
- Hebrews 12:1-13—An encouragement to follow the example of Jesus in pursuing purity.
- 1 Peter 3:13-17—Peter's exhortation is really an appeal for Christians to be moral champions in the workplace.

Reading
Hyde, Douglas. *Dedication and Leadership.* Notre Dame, Ind.: University of Notre Dame Press, 1966.

Projects
1. If you know some other Christians where you work, get together and begin praying and discussing how God might use you to influence coworkers for Christ.
2. Plan a meeting or luncheon on some workplace topic and invite everyone in your organization or network to come. Suggested subjects: stress, success, integrity and ethics, balancing work and family. Announce ahead of time that the speaker will offer insights from the Bible on the issue. Be sure to find a speaker who (a) knows the issue, (b) knows the Scripture on that issue, (c) can communicate biblical truth clearly, appropriately, and practically to nonChristians, and (d) has an unimpeachable reputation in the community.

NOTES: 1. Douglas Hyde, *Dedication and Leadership* (Notre Dame, Ind.: University of Notre Dame Press, 1966), pages 156-157.
2. Hyde, page 157.
3. Doug Sherman and William Hendricks, *Your Work Matters to God* (Colorado Springs, Colo.: NavPress, 1987), page 241.

You Can Make an Impact!

In session 15 we asked you to consider your influence on non-Christians in your network. But Christians also need encouragement and challenge to live out their beliefs on the job.

Our research indicates that more than ninety percent of the Christians in America have *never* heard a sermon, read a book, listened to a tape, or otherwise been exposed to teaching that relates practical, biblical principles to the issues they face every day on the job! That means that if you've come this far in our book and in this study guide, you've already had far more input than most of the other Christians you know! *Now you can influence them with a vision for how their work and life matter to God!*

In this session we want you to consider at least one strategy for helping Christians in your network, the small discussion group. Our hope is that you'll use that strategy to make an impact for Christ where you work.

THE NEEDS OF CHRISTIAN WORKERS

Every Christian in the marketplace has at least four needs:

- to be known, accepted, and understood;
- to be inspired to moral excellence;
- to have resources for decision-making and problem-solving;
- to have resources for growing in Christlikeness on the job.

109

Discussion
1. Which of these needs do you especially feel?

2. Make a list of as many Christians as you can think of on your job and in your occupational or professional network.

3. Put a check by the names of people with whom you already have more than a casual relationship, or with whom you think you could develop a close relationship.

4. Thinking of the names you checked, which of the needs listed on page 109 do these Christians have?

A STRATEGY FOR IMPACT

One of the most effective ways we have seen for Christians to meet their needs on the job is to get together and discuss specific work-place issues and try to apply biblical principles to them. (Even getting together with *one* other Christian on a regular basis to talk about common issues and to pray together is a *valuable* discipline.) We explain the advantages of this approach and how to get started in chapter 16 of our book, and we recommend you review that material before you actually implement the strategy that follows.

5. a. The people whose names you checked in question 3 above are good possibilities to participate in some form of regular discussion. Which of them would you be willing to approach with this idea?

   b. Now pull out your calendar or appointment book and decide when you will contact them about their participation.

   c. When you do contact each one, explain the basic purpose of the group and invite them to an initial meeting.
      Also suggest two or three possible times when you

could hold the first meeting. Having some suggested times gives your prospects something definite to respond to. After you get some idea of who wants to be there and when they are available, you can finalize the date in your calendar.

d. Remind each person a day or two before your initial meeting. Be sure each one knows the exact time and place for the meeting.

e. Keep the following in mind at the first meeting:

- Make sure everyone is introduced.
- Explain the basic purpose of the group and how you envision it will function. Then allow everyone there to modify your proposal until you reach a consensus as to the purpose, format, and expectations for the group. Our recommendation is to ask people for only a six-week commitment at any one time.
- Begin discussing a specific issue. If you bring a brief case history or a useful set of statistics or quotes, this will likely get things rolling. You may want to use one of the sessions in this study guide as a starter.
- End on time! People have other commitments. Don't be afraid to cut off a lively discussion.
- Set a time and place for the next discussion.

A Word of Caution

We've had considerable experience, both positive and negative, in small group discussion. Our advice is, *keep your expectations simple.* If you do, you will likely enjoy a handful of very positive, very powerful experiences with other believers. It's amazing what the Spirit of God can do when His people come together to consider how Christ and His Word make a difference in the everyday world of work.

FOR FURTHER STUDY

Scripture
- Proverbs 11:14—Describes the value of seeking godly counsel.

• James 5:16—A passage that affirms the value of small groups of Christians who pray for one another.

Projects
1. If you are an executive, consider using Career Impact Ministries' *Standing Out in Your Workplace* discussion materials with a small group of your peers. This series of case-study discussions of workplace issues is a lay-led approach to helping Christians put their faith to work in the marketplace. For more information on these resources, contact CIM, P.O. Box 5030, Arlington, TX 76005, or call toll-free 1-800-4-IMPACT.
2. If you want to create an interest among other Christians in how Christianity applies to work, give them copies of books such as *Your Work Matters to God,* R.C. Sproul's *Stronger Than Steel,* or Jack Eckerd's *The Right Prescription.* Make an effort to discuss the books with those who read them.

BIBLE STUDY MATERIALS FROM NAVPRESS

BIBLE STUDY SERIES
DESIGN FOR DISCIPLESHIP—seven books and leader's guide
EXPERIENCING GOD—two books
GOD IN YOU—six books and leader's guide
GOD'S DESIGN FOR THE FAMILY—two books
LEARNING TO LIVE—six books
LIFECHANGE—studies of books of the Bible
STUDIES IN CHRISTIAN LIVING—six books

TOPICAL BIBLE STUDIES
Becoming a Woman of Excellence
The Blessing Study Guide
Celebrate the Seasons!
The Creator, My Confidant
Growing in Christ
Growing Strong in God's Family
Healing the Broken Places
Homemaking
Justice
Leadership
A Mother's Legacy
The New Mothers Guide
On Holy Ground
Political Action
Saints, Sinners, and a Sovereign God—and leader's guide
To Walk and Not Grow Weary
Transforming Society
When the Squeeze Is On

BIBLE STUDIES WITH COMPANION BOOKS
The Freedom of Obedience
Inside Out
Living for What Really Matters
The Practice of Godliness
The Pursuit of Holiness
Trusting God
Your Work Matters to God

RESOURCES
How to Lead Small Group Bible Studies
Jesus Cares for Women
The Navigator Bible Studies Handbook
Topical Memory System—available in KJV/NIV and NASB/RSV
Your Home, A Lighthouse